ZORAN VIDOVIĆ

HOW TO LEAD, INSPIRE AND DEVELOP HUMAN DIGNITY

A practical leadership guide for building ethical, efficient,
and high-performing teams, without the fluff.

I0080466

Leadership: "Profound Leadership Considerations."
Human Resources: "A Guide to Understanding Why."
Entrepreneurship: "The Reasons Behind Failure!"

2025

Copyright Disclaimer

To my Dragana, Mauro, and Ramona.
You made me the leader I am today.

Acknowledgment

I wrote the initial manuscript in December 2023, and then it took me another two years to publish it. A journey of growth and development supported by my loved ones, who endured late evenings and long hours of solitude and focus.

So, a huge thank you goes to my family, who supported me when needed and pushed me forward when I got stuck.

A special thank you goes to my dear friend Anthony S., who supported me with the initial proofreading and editing. His insights, grounded in extensive experience helped shape and elevate my early drafts and strengthen this book's voice.

Another invaluable partner in this endeavor is my dear friend Ivan K., who provided honest and thoughtful feedback on the final manuscript. His perspective as a reader and subject expert helped me add visual aids and explanations.

Also, a big thank you goes to my editorial and publishing team for their exceptional service.

Thank you all for making it happen.

TABLE OF CONTENTS

Author's Note

Throughout my career, I have been privileged with opportunities for personal development in various industries, starting with the hospitality industry, which has greatly influenced my communication and problem-solving skills. My professional growth took me in the military direction, where I further developed as an officer and exploited my abilities in understanding and leading people while utilizing available resources to achieve the set mission. I further widened my skill set with close protection skills and enrolled in the marine security segment of the cruise industry, which provided a great environment rich in diverse cultures, personal beliefs, and interpersonal challenges, enriching me as a skilled professional in understanding people, processes and technology.

Accumulated knowledge and experience, complemented by a bachelor's degree in economics, have greatly served me in becoming an entrepreneur within the hospitality real estate industry.

My professional journey has exposed me to a variety of environments, circumstances, procedures, protocols, processes, tools, systems, equipment, challenges, and conflicts, but it all taught me to understand the importance of humans across all industries, along with their abilities, in relation to a fragile balance between the environments complementing and boosting performance and those destroying it. The common denominator is leadership style, which is fragile and dependent on environmental influence combined with the leader's character and personality.

During my career, I have had opportunities to work with people displaying a variety of behaviors underlined in this book. Some of my commanders and leaders were up to the task with complementing leadership abilities and positive leadership styles. Unfortunately, there were far too many others who adopted leadership styles that destroyed any possibility of growth and development, leaving people constantly chasing the "carrot."

I have also met and led a variety of people within the soldier and employee cohort, with both superior and limited abilities and motivation, which helped me develop and fine-tune approaches for each individual.

This all fascinates me as sometimes the resolution to a presented challenge, although within reach and easily implemented, cannot be implemented due to a lack of understanding or the will to do so by the responsible individuals. It is a perplexing and extraordinary phenomenon that grabbed my attention early on. It is a phenomenon that is shaping the world we know and influencing our lives, with the majority of people not even realizing it.

Thank you for showing interest in this phenomenon, and let's dive together into the abyss of human behaviors. I'm looking forward to receiving feedback and your personal experiences on the subject matter.

Preface

What is the most important asset of a successful company? Well, obviously, it is not technology but rather humans executing tasks and making decisions. This brings us to a staggering revelation of how our personal limitations have a deep impact on our performance, which is evident from the catastrophic statistics showing 96% of maritime accidents caused by human error, along with 88% of aviation accidents.[1][2]

So, what is the cause? Fatigue? System adoption failure? Not enough training? Poor leadership? Flawed hiring processes? Or perhaps a combination of the above?

We can put in place various systems to assist with selected processes and help minimize human error, but we cannot eliminate it completely. Along with the technology, we can put in place tailored procedures with clear goals and simple, non-dubious structures, but it is most important to have the right person for the right job, which, as easy and logical as it seems, turns out to be the hardest task yet.

For us to even try to achieve that, we will need to look into the cultural, economic, and political influences on the operation. We will also need to be honest with ourselves and identify our own flaws first to be able to address the same in others. This

---

1. https://www.marineinsight.com/marine-safety/the-relation-between-human-error-and-marine-industry/#:~:text=These%20studies%20were%20aimed%20at%20finding%20out%20root,the%20reason%20for%20maritime%20accidents%20was%20human%20error.

2. https://www.faasafety.gov/files/gslac/courses/content/258/1097/AMT_Handbook_Addendum_Human_Factors.pdf

is a challenging job, as self-reflection and critique are a virtue not cherished by many. This book is not a comprehensive instruction book but rather an overview of the structure that most companies have. However, the focus of this book is on the importance of humans in the great scheme of things. We are going to discuss different segments of a company and try to scratch the surface of human behaviors contributing to failures and potentially catastrophic events.

We are going to establish processes helping to self-reflect and correct our approach to leading others. We will provide insight for the entrepreneurs, leaders, and the rest of the employees to understand the right approach to motivating, adjusting, and elevating performance. The tool that will help establish minimum standards against which we can measure and scrutinize performance for all levels of business, ranging from a small business to a corporation.

CHAPTER 1
Management or Leadership?

There seems to be a misconception that management and leadership are the same. Although they are interconnected and deeply dependent on each other, we need to understand the differences to be able to excel in both.

Management is the process of aligning all available resources with the company's mission and vision while also reflecting on and identifying opportunities for growth and change in alignment with positive trends and interests of society.

Leadership is the process of inspiring your subordinates to align with the company's mission and vision while adhering to the highest standards in achieving the best possible result by creating opportunities for their self-development and growth.

True leaders create new leaders and are not intimidated by employees with high potential, as they see it as an opportunity to develop new leaders who will serve the company and society.

The above are predominantly separated in larger enterprises where managers are not necessarily directly involved in leadership roles; however, leaders are most likely also involved in management roles. Every leader who is in charge of a team of people is also in charge of certain processes and equipment with set goals to achieve.

So, we can conclude that the two are interconnected as a leadership role comes out of a management role, with a focus on humans.

This is quite clear for larger enterprises, but it is not the case for small businesses where a "one-man band" is more of a rule than an exception. That is where the friction might arise, as the need to be on top of all the processes and then be required to inspire, motivate, train, and lead people in the desired direction of the company's mission and vision can be overwhelming. It is an exhausting process that takes a lot of time and energy, especially for entrepreneurs in a start-up phase.

That is why it is important to understand the crucial role of leadership in the management process, as humans are going to make it or break it for you.

To achieve this balance, one needs to understand all the elements and processes needed for a business to succeed, regardless of being an entrepreneur or a leader.

This is imperative to be able to understand and align yourself and all employees with the company's mission and vision, provided they are anchored in ethical principles serving the greater good and society.

CHAPTER 2
Defining your company's mission and vision

2.1 The mission

Every business starts with an idea that is then passed through the thought process and tested against projected market requirements. This then becomes a potent idea, and further energy is invested in the execution. Obviously, none of it makes any sense if we do not understand the market we are getting into and do not have an idea of which segment of the market we plan to cover and, more importantly, why.

Why are we engaging in entrepreneurship, and what are our goals? Are we serving the greater good of society, or is our motive pure monetary gain?

For example, if we are getting into the hospitality market, we need to understand the industry standard and decide what positive impact we are going to have on it. How are we going to stand out and attract customers? What are we going to offer more of, or perhaps somewhat differently, from competitors? Have we identified guest desires and needs that haven't been satisfied by other companies, or are we planning to offer the prevailing industry products and services but with a focus on excellence? Have we identified opportunities for improving and elevating employee satisfaction in the industry, which will reflect on guest satisfaction and subsequently our bottom line?

Let's say we are going to enter the hospitality real estate market in the Mediterranean. We are going to look into market offerings and demand. We can do this by exploring the web or by meeting with rental agents and receiving feedback on demand and which part of the market is not yet covered. What is there a shortage of? Is it hotels or private accommodations? Is it villas that are in higher demand? If so, in what capacity and what level of luxury is desired? What are the challenges the industry is facing? What level of services are we planning to offer? How are we going to serve society with our business? Are we going to have a positive impact on the community and the environment? Then we are going to revisit our original idea and adjust it to suit the current and possible projected market needs. We will obviously take our budget into consideration and decide if we are able to stay within our limits to make sure we are profitable while not compromising our mission.

Our mission: *"We create unforgettable memories for our guests while sustainably embracing the local culture and tradition."*

2.2 The vision

Our mission is to provide the best products and services for our guests while serving our community.

Now we need to identify how we are going to position our company in the market to achieve it in a set time frame. Are we going to go down the road of being "green" and "environmentally friendly" or perhaps use some other approach tailored to grabbing people's attention, such as focusing on everyone's well-being and cherishing local tradition? Are we going to focus on service excellence, hoping it will speak for itself and get recognized by the targeted audience? Are we going to achieve excellence by empowering and including our employees in the process? Whatever we choose, we will need to do some research and identify what makes some businesses stand out and achieve stronger market position than others. What are they offering that is different from the rest of the market? What are they excelling in? How can we outperform that and offer more appealing and rewarding products or services? How can we positively influence our employees and society? It is most important to have a goal other than pure financial gain, which is fundamental for every business and will distinguish us from the rest of the market and serve our society.

Our vision: *"By 2030 we will redefine the hospitality industry by delivering unforgettable guest experiences that celebrate and embrace local culture and tradition, benefiting our employees, the environment and society."*

Both the mission and vision are our guiding principles, as they provide direction by setting clear goals and defining a time frame to achieve them.

Obviously, this will all depend on the type of business we are engaging in. The law firm, the bank, and the oil company will obviously focus on different approaches with different goals, as they are competing in completely different markets. Based on all this, we will have a clear idea of our company's mission, along with a vision of where we want to see our company within a certain time period.

Whatever path we choose, we need to understand that success will depend on our employees, and it is our leadership's responsibility to create a climate where employees can thrive and bring results. This needs to be embedded in both our mission and vision. It is imperative, as they will pass on enthusiasm and energy to potential clients by capturing their attention and subsequently selling our products or services.

Great examples and very well dissected in the book Isus Lider *by Vladimir Grebenar.*

2.3 Decision influences

We need to understand that this approach will also depend on current political and social conditions dictated by prominent political and media leaders. It is essential to understand the business climate and potential shift in social consensus predominantly directed by media influencers. Why media? Well, whoever controls the media has access to people's minds, especially in this day and age where technology has become an integrated part of our lives with instant information flow. History has shown us many negative examples of media power, from 1940s Germany to the 2020 pandemic, where the prevailing social consensus was suspended and even canceled. Recent history has taught us that, unfortunately, consumers have very short memories, as a whole, and can easily be diverted from the facts toward the projected self-generated positive image volunteered by guilty companies. The pharmaceutical, along with automobile, oil, and chemical companies, are prime examples of an image repair and public focus shift from catastrophes toward potential heroes. This would not be possible without media engagement, as well as political blessing. It provides an opportunity to understand the importance of situational awareness in regard to the influences of power.

Pharmaceutical companies have paid enormous settlements and fines due to their wrongdoing by either misleading consumers or paying bribes to officials and medical doctors. One example is Pfizer with a $2.3 billion settlement, as disclosed by the U.S. Justice Department on September 2nd, 2009, for misbranding Bextra (an anti-inflammatory drug) with the intent to defraud or mislead.[3]

Another one is Johnson & Johnson paying $2.2 billion to resolve criminal and civil investigations, as reported by the U.S. Justice Department on November 4th, 2013, regarding the allegations involving the prescription drugs Risperdal, Invega, and Natrecor. Those drugs were promoted for uses not approved as safe and effective by the Food and Drug Administration, along with payments of kickbacks to certain physicians and the nation's largest long-term care pharmacy provider.[45]

AstraZeneca is not a stranger to similar practices; as announced by the U.S. Justice Department on April 27th, 2010, AstraZencca was ordered to pay $520 million to resolve allegations of Off-label Drug Marketing.[6]

Now, fast-forward almost a decade, and those three companies are on the pedestal for the new Covid-19 therapy, administered with a syringe. They are now considered trustworthy to the extent of being trusted with drug development using new technology, never before used for treating humans, in an expedited time frame. Obviously, success will guarantee a substantial financial reward, along with propelling the companies to the top of the market. This

---

3. https://www.justice.gov/opa/pr/justice-department-announces-largest-health-care-fraud-settlement-its-history

4. https://www.justice.gov/opa/pr/johnson-johnson-pay-more-22-billion-resolve-criminal-and-civil-investigations

5. https://www.merriam-webster.com/dictionary/kickback

6. https://www.justice.gov/opa/pr/pharmaceutical-giant-astrazeneca-pay-520-million-label-drug-marketing

is perhaps not something we should easily allow to happen for any company, especially not for those with a history of misleading practices. Well, the media hype and political trust, run by interests, along with the "science" community turning a blind eye, and our candidates managed to get their products established as the "holy grail" and only solution, ignoring any other point of view, including the renowned scientists in the same field of medicine and pharmacy. A sense of urgency creates a tunnel vision in political and emergency response groups, creating compelling grounds for decision-making fueled by necessity and self-preservation disguised as being in the best interest of society. This is understandable, to an extent, as in any emergency, people make decisions with the information they have at that point in time, and they often rely on "authority" in a relevant discipline to have something to fall back on and then be able to say that they just followed the science. So, they often trade competency for complacency wrapped in a false sense of security and protection under an umbrella of like-minded opinions supported by the interests of large, influential groups.

The above is specific for the big players, and there is a reason behind it. The company gradually grows and transforms from a non-living organization into a self-guided, semi-live entity. What does it mean? It means that the company has become too large or valuable to be left to the market laws, and it is protected by its supporters, both from the inside and outside. It could be that the company is considered prominent and leading in its industry and so worth special attention and treatment, or it is considered potent and possibly the only solution to the perceived threat, such as during the 2020 pandemic. Sometimes, it is the share size of the company that warrants attention and actions from its political supporters, as its failure is deemed too hazardous to their interests. We have examples of bailouts across industries where millions of jobs have been preserved.[7] Either way, it will enjoy protection from political partners in tailoring an environment supporting the company's final goal by painting a public image of integrity, ingenuity, and necessity, with a tendency to eliminate any signals suggesting the opposite. By doing so, we have given life to the company as it is treated almost like a living entity with special treatment, allowing it to become self-guided, focusing on its success irrespective of whether its actions are in line with the interests of society.

This then puts the company on a trajectory complementing its final goal: profit, without consideration of the possible obstacles in achieving it. It is apparent with all big companies that allow themselves to influence people's lives to an extent when new generations cannot live without their products or services. This is a pivot point when a company turns from a non-living into a semi-live entity. Such a condition usually materializes during or just after a major crisis where a certain need is satisfied by the selected provider, making its products essential for the future or by a technical development accepted by the masses, which then becomes essential for society.

Throughout history, harsh times have introduced nail-on solutions that are still used today, ranging from synthetic rubber to microwaves, duct tape, and a Jeep. Modern days have brought us online stores, which exponentially grew during the 2020 pandemic-imposed lockdowns and movement restrictions. Some of the companies emerged as absolute leaders in their industry, like Amazon and Pfizer, by demonstrating readiness to adjust to the market shift, not to mention the IT sector, which

---

7. https://www.investopedia.com/articles/economics/08/government-financial-bailout.asp

has the advantage of being flexible and not restricted by location and time, but rather by internet access.

We are currently living in a world inconceivable to our ancestors as the world has become one small playground for the big companies. Companies so large that they change and, to an extent, dictate people's lives and influence political decisions and lawmaking.

This is important to understand when we are exploring the opportunities to enter certain markets, regardless of the size of our investment. We need to be conscious of our abilities, our vision, and the market circumstances, developing a clear understanding of market trends, along with the strengths and weaknesses of our competitors. It is important to understand those forces influencing the market that have the potential to boost our competitors and leave us swimming upstream.

We also need to understand that political reach will affect our bottom line, as "government money" is only a term since it is public money generated by taxing the public. We need to look into taxation and the possibility of new taxes being introduced. For example, if you have invested in the Croatian rental market and built villas prior to 2025, you were not required to pay property tax, as there wasn't one in Croatia. This was changed, and property tax was introduced on January 1st, 2025, although it has been unsuccessfully attempted before by previous governments. There are also differences between the tax liabilities for locals and foreigners, which we need to be aware of, as foreigners are obliged to pay VAT on all the services they have provided, while the rental businesses owned by Croatian residents are only required to pay the service fee charged by rental agencies operating outside Croatia. Local rental owners will also need to pay VAT on all their services if the yearly income limit is surpassed. There is also tax imposed by the local municipal council depending on the type and size of the accommodation, along with mandatory fees paid to the Croatian National Tourist Board. So, the above is valuable information to consider as it will greatly influence the bottom line, along with the fact the Croatian government adopted the Euro in 2023, which skyrocketed living expenses along with labor prices. This is very important as, for example, the price of cleaning services has doubled in a couple of years due to extensive market expansion, along with elevated living expenses. Croatia entering the Eurozone resulted in the workforce becoming scarce, as Croatians decided to enter the employment markets of other European countries with better living standards. This is also boosting labor prices and, more importantly, shrinking the skilled labor force, especially in the hospitality industry. The Croatian government then decided to import foreign workers, which presented additional challenges with the language barrier, along with associated cultural differences. Also, real estate demand has increased, and subsequently, this has elevated real estate prices.

Obviously, all of this is something we can have minimum influence on, but we need to be aware of it to make informed and timely decisions, especially if we are entering markets heavily influenced by the above. We might decide it is not worth the time and effort, or perhaps that it is, in which case it is preparing us for the expected challenges.

Either way, we will have greater chances to come to an informed decision based on the facts and not just wishful thinking. That's why it is important to be critical and to make sure we check and analyze all information received from various sources to be able to determine the status quo.

2.4 Avoiding flawed systems

We can find good examples of success in a variety of industries, along with examples of flawed structure and management leading to incompetence and complacency, resulting in catastrophe. So, we need to identify the same and work toward establishing the company within our selected market while focusing on setting working ethics and competency as a primary drive fueled by ingenuity and striving for excellence. This helps produce and maintain high-quality products and services, which are then recognized by the consumers. It also prevents complacency and incompetence from embedding deeply in our teams, not allowing them to become cancer, slowly eating away at competency, innovation, and ingenuity, resulting in potential catastrophes.

We have had opportunities to witness and, unfortunately, to be affected by poor and criminal decisions made by mediocre politicians and company leaders focused solely on their own self-interest. There is a long list of companies that have disappointed, misled, and betrayed consumers. These may start with the oil companies' catastrophic disasters, including off-shore, tankers, and pipeline disasters, which negatively affected the environment and subsequently flora, fauna, and all the people living in the affected areas.[8] Those catastrophes also affect people in different industries such as fishing and tourism, as their source of income is now negatively impacted, or even eliminated in the damaged areas.

Then we have examples from the pharmaceutical industry, which has proven itself to be deeply tainted.[9] The list of

---

8. https://en.wikipedia.org/wiki/List_of_oil_spills
9. https://en.wikipedia.org/wiki/

companies and incidents is appalling, with billions of dollars paid as settlements due to foul play. Those companies continue to enjoy people's trust, as well as the full support of political parties, bolstering them with favorable decisions. The kickback seems to be the preferred choice for the pharmaceutical industry. This is, obviously, all done with the help of lobbying groups, both within government agencies and from doctors.

The chemical industry is also a big polluter and has inflicted negative impacts on people's lives, as well as flora and fauna.[10] There are examples of wrongdoing by the chemical companies, which were penalized by courts of law and have ended up issuing enormous settlements.[11] But this is just a fraction of the price to pay. There are still hundreds of billions of dollars of environmental damage that are being financed by taxpayer money.

The automobile industry is not a stranger to fraudulent practices, as demonstrated by Volkswagen in the 2015 diesel engine fraud scandal. VW reported $18 billion in losses in 2015 due to the cost of fines, recalls, and legal claims, as reported by the *New York Times*.[12]

We should not forget the 2008 U.S. housing crisis, which sums it all up as the preeminent example of how these sorts of practices adversely impact American lives.[13] It is a story of mergers and growth in the banking sector with expanding influences resulting in political support in interpreting existing

List_of_largest_pharmaceutical_settlements

10. https://www.epa.gov/pfas/pfas-explained

11. https://www.theguardian.com/environment/2023/aug/03/chemical-companies-pfas-payouts-forever-chemicals

12. https://www.nytimes.com/2016/04/23/business/international/volkswagen-loss-emissions-scandal.html

13. https://en.wikipedia.org/wiki/Subprime_mortgage_crisis

laws, and introducing new laws, complementing desired growth within the sector, while maintaining a narrow vision and ignorance as a widespread rule, emphatically not an isolated approach.

All of the above leads us to conclude that regardless of the financial impact imposed on those guilty companies, due to their share size and enormous financial wealth backed up by lobbyists securing relevant government support, they are not always deeply affected. There seem to be few repercussions for the top decision-makers within those companies as well as responsible government agencies, which leads us to believe there could be a flawed system in place as if there are "phantom" decision-makers who are solely responsible but unknown, and so out of reach of the law. There could be repercussions for the lower-level management or the cohort within executing fraud, but the upper levels, along with the monitoring segments, do not seem to be affected, nor do they learn from it, which subsequently leaves the door open for similar practices. This helps the status quo, and the modus operandi stays the same as the repercussions do not appear to be severe enough for the true decision-makers.

Now the question is: How is all this possible? Well, it is due to humans "just doing their job." A good example is the VW diesel engine fraud case where, as reported by the U.S. Department of Justice on August 25th, 2017, a VW engineer was sentenced to 40 months in federal prison, with two years of supervised release, for his role in a nearly 10-year conspiracy to defraud U.S. regulators and Volkswagen customers. [14] The interesting fact is the defendant had testified that he had been tasked by VW, to develop the defeat device in order to cheat

---

14. https://www.justice.gov/opa/pr/volkswagen-engineer-sentenced-his-role-conspiracy-cheat-us-emissions-tests

U.S. emissions tests. The defendant and his co-conspirators falsely and fraudulently certified VW diesel vehicles with EPA and CARB, so they complied with the Clean Air Act and met U.S. emission standards.

Any individual who follows instructions without running them through their personal value system is part of the problem and, unfortunately, fuels the self-guided, semi-live company's goal. Anyone working in a large organization, regardless of whether it is a government or private entity, has had the opportunity to meet self-centered, highly ambitious individuals willing to do anything to make it to the top. Now, these individuals help bring the self-guided, semi-live company to life. They are the fuel, stripped of any compassion, and with their personal goals ahead, they are willing to obey to reach them. The scary part is that they do attain their goals, and then the sky is the limit with disasters waiting to happen.

This sounds like an example of a narcissistic, sociopathic, or even psychopathic personality and, to an extent, it probably is. It appears as if most people in power trade some of their compassion and moral filters for the stone-cold, submissive, obedient persona devoid of any character to fit the required profile for the position while being rewarded with desired compensation. Looking at these powerful and influential people, one might suspect they are all cut from the same cloth. Well, it appears as if it comes with the territory, as power is the ultimate rush and has been the ambition of many generations and will be for the generations to come.

So, we need to be aware of it as it will affect our businesses, too. We need to make sure we are ready to prevent it and cut it out at its roots once detected. We need to establish a culture and environment that do not support that kind of behavior and allow for the early detection of any deviation from the company's standards, mission, and vision. We also need to understand the inevitable reality of growth and expansion with the challenges pertaining to maintaining the set standard and work ethics. We can easily maintain such set standards when we run one small operation under our personal supervision. The challenge begins with our expansion as we need to delegate jobs and assign responsibility, trusting that the same standard is going to be adhered to. Well, this is where we are at risk of failing if we do not understand human nature and its fallibilities. It is like playing Chinese whispers, and the more people play it, the greater the chance of information loss.

For this reason, it is imperative to establish the culture, standards, and processes supporting and maintaining the company's mission and vision and prevent personal influences from diluting the process and diverting it for personal gain.

CHAPTER 3
Establishing a business legal framework

3.1 Identifying rules and regulations

What does this mean? Well, after deciding on the company's mission and vision, we want to make sure we can achieve all the set goals while being in line with all the applicable laws and regulations. If we decide we want to put out a public image of a "green" and "environmentally friendly" company, we will first need to identify what is required to be able to achieve that. What is the industry standard and requirement for it? How much time, money, and effort is it going to require, and how can we minimize the expense and maximize the benefit of such a market position? Are there any new laws in the pipeline that might influence our operation in the future? Any new regulations being considered? Any push from prominent large industry leaders toward regulation updates to support their desired industry positions? We will need to hire competent and inquisitive people who will guide us in the right direction and provide accurate and independent advice while keeping focus on current and future trends.

We can also hire a third party to take responsibility for this part of the process to ensure we are in line and not at risk of breaking any applicable laws and regulations and to provide advice in positioning the company in line with future trends.

This might involve getting ahead of the curve and perhaps implementing expected changes ahead of time to establish the working culture and minimize the impact on the employees and operation once the new regulations are introduced. It leaves us with enough time to run the operation under elevated regulations to simulate the expected changes and help discover the operational and financial impact, along with opportunities for improvement, without risking fines.

Obviously, this aspect of our operation will be dynamic and ever-evolving, depending on our industry, with change being more of a rule than an exception. With company growth, we will need to have a complementing department of people monitoring, assessing, and predicting future trends while keeping an eye on the industry and our competitors. This segment of the company will guide us in the desired direction in line with all applicable laws and regulations and sound the alarm on any discovery of any deviation. One thing we do not need is blindly obedient employees focused on ascending the ranks regardless of the tactics. We will need to have comprehensive and clear policies and processes that prevent us from hiring and maintaining a team of individuals focusing solely on self-interest at the expense of the company's goal.

3.2 Risk management; setting and maintaining direction to support the company's mission

This segment of our company is crucial for maintaining proper direction toward our set mission and protecting the company. This does not mean we will not stay up-to-date with the market trends as well as the legal frameworks, but it means we will always maintain the desired direction, supported by the strict standard of not allowing complacency and political or social trends to negatively influence our company's mission and vision while keeping the focus on sustainable growth and development.

We have witnessed the shift away from the traditional direction in the auto industry under political and social influence, all enflamed by the media and forced "correctness" and fueled by EV subsidies and tax exemptions. It has led to a determination to abandon the conventional approach and turn toward the new "sustainable" electric cars within the set deadline regardless of the cost or the potential risk of failure since it appears the technology and the infrastructure are still not there to actually sustain it. This has been identified by the survey conducted on 330,000 vehicles reported by Consumer Reports in November 2024.[15] The survey analyzed car models within the last three years, with data suggesting the hybrids are as reliable as traditional gas vehicles compared to electric vehicles which reportedly have 42% more problems, along with plug-in hybrids having 70% more problems than gas vehicles. This is a positive change and a big step forward compared to the survey results from 2023. Now, does the tendency to shift and to explore other technologies, such as electric cars, have its place in industry? Of course, it does. There are also other unconventional technologies being explored, such as hydrogen vehicles using an internal combustion engine and hydrogen fuel cell vehicles, all with specific advantages and limitations. Issues might arise when you blatantly ignore facts and decide on a direction that could potentially put the company at risk. Toyota is a positive example of a cautious and diversified approach to net zero emissions with an array of solutions ranging from

---

15. https://www.consumerreports.org/
cars/car-reliability-owner-satisfaction/
electric-vehicles-are-less-reliable-than-conventional-cars-a1047214174/

hybrid full electric to the current development of hydrogen engines. They are obviously conscious of all the challenges and limitations of EV vehicles as they have extensive experience with that technology. We have seen car manufacturers scaling down their electrification plans in 2024 and 2025, as reported by Reuters and Business Insider, due to a drop in demand.[16] [17] This comes after their initial commitment to go fully electric, which shows signals of misalignment between vision and reality.

Great responsibility also lies on the politicians due to their tendency to impose regulations forcing global change within set time frames without taking fully into consideration potential negative impacts and the feasibility of regulation implementation across the industry. An interesting example is the EU's CO_2 emission regulation for 2025, which is now resulting in automobile companies collaborating in a CO_2 emission credit trade with full EV companies, such as Tesla, to avoid fines, according to Reuters.[18] So, we are witnessing a shift of power in the market, created by a legislation, which is now pocketing a 3% income to EV company just due to CO_2 emission credit trade.

We have seen examples of wrongdoing and misleading practices within the auto industry even prior to this tectonic shift, with the prime example being the VW 2015 diesel engine emission fraud scandal. Obviously, we should not be so naïve as to think that similar practices will not be attempted by desperate companies addressing the newly imposed CO_2

---

16. https://www.reuters.com/business/autos-transportation/carmakers-adjust-electrification-plans-ev-demand-slows-2024-09-06/

17. https://www.businessinsider.com/automakers-rolling-back-electric-car-plans-porsche-honda-jeep-ford-2025-9#ford-6

18. https://www.reuters.com/business/autos-transportation/stellantis-toyota-ford-mazda-subaru-plan-pool-co2-emissions-with-tesla-2025-01-07/

regulations and electric car challenges. We've had the chance to witness the limitations of those products, along with the shortcomings of the supporting infrastructure in Chicago, as reported by the *New York Times* on January 17th, 2024. People got stranded at electric vehicle charging stations due to freezing cold temperatures negatively affecting the technology, causing deviations from the advertised levels of performance. [19] And no, we should not abandon new technologies nor stop developing them, but we need to understand the limitations and admit the shortcomings to address them and minimize the impact on society and the environment that we are trying to save. We can take sides in the debate and support or oppose the product and new legislation, but we must remember that our perspective would differ if we were stranded in the freezing cold with perhaps a sick or pregnant family member in the car. So, the personal impact changes people's perception of the product, probably for good, which is not something we should take lightly as they might become advocates against it. This is why it is not wise to jeopardize the set standard in delivering excellence and ingenuity. We need to advance down the path of change once all the risks and benefits are identified, analyzed, and addressed. We also need to understand our consumers with all their desires and expectations as they will direct us onto a desired path of success. We need to understand that our consumers are the fuel of our economy, and we should avoid getting in the mindset that we can easily change the consumer's desires and needs in a short period of time to suit any sudden turns of our desired direction. That can backfire very quickly, leaving us backpedaling and trying to retrieve the lost trust, which can be costly and sometimes impossible to do. People are creatures of

---

19. https://www.nytimes.com/2024/01/17/business/tesla-charging-chicago-cold-weather.html

habit with the tendency to reward trust to companies providing products and services satisfying their needs at their desired standard. People also tend to identify with and take ownership of their desired products with a refusal to accept change unless the change is convenient and somewhat desired, so we need to feel the beat of our consumers' aspirations.

A recent reminder is the 2025 "Cracker Barrel Old Country Store" logo and menu change in the US, which resulted in negative publicity and strong pushback from customers, particularly conservatives, causing the company's stock price to drop by $10 in a single day. It also prompted a public reaction from sitting US President Donald Trump, who advised leveraging negative publicity and reverting to the old logo, a step that the company ultimately took.[20]

Now, you might wonder what the legal framework has to do with this. Well, a big part of it is risk management, which should maintain the direction of minimizing the risk taken and have all the boxes ticked before decisions are made. The mission is key, and the business legal framework makes you stay in the lane. It minimizes risk, whether it comes from outside elements, such as new laws or a lawsuit against us, or from the inside, such as decisions taking the company away from its mission and potentially open to scrutiny. That being said, we also need to be cautious not to create a culture where all ingenuity is traded away for the perception of safety and preservation, not allowing us to get in line with positive trends and explore the technological or operational advancements successfully implemented by our competitors. We have examples of companies going bankrupt by not aligning with technology advancement and believing in their superiority with the mindset: "We have always done it

20. https://www.usatoday.com/story/money/2025/08/27/cracker-barrel-logo-change-timeline/85845032007/_

this way." Kodak is a prime example of an ultimate price paid for not recognizing opportunities for change and growth in line with new technologies.

If we want to reach the top and stay there, we will need to embrace excellence and ingenuity at our core. These must be our foundation and not traded away at any cost. This is a continuous process as times change, and we need to make sure we keep up with positive trends without jeopardizing our excellence, ingenuity, and the company's mission while allowing for a visionary approach to detecting opportunities for improvement.

It is imperative to have a good reputation and to build credibility. This is done by fair play and striving for excellence while building know-how and an appropriate culture supporting the company's goals. It takes time to build the standard, but it can be ruined quickly, so we need to maintain it and look for ways of improving it in line with positive trends. We need to have a clear and comprehensive set of procedures and processes with complementary training to achieve and maintain the desired standard.

3.3 Communicating with the public

Public relations are deeply connected to and greatly influence legal and risk management factors. We are living in a new millennium where the information flow is imminent, regardless of the information source or credibility. This can negatively affect any organization and, if not taken care of immediately, can have a deep impact. One can wonder why this is relevant. We can look into a prime example of how far things can go when taken too far and out of context by looking at the case of Gibson's Bakery vs. Oberlin College in the USA.[21] The court ruled in favor of Gibson's Bakery and awarded tens of millions of dollars to be paid by the Oberlin College due to "libel, intentional infliction of emotional distress and intentional interference with a business relationship" as reported by the *New York Times*. This was all triggered by Gibson's Bakery stopping a student from shoplifting. This then triggered the student community to protest and subsequently resulted in a boycott supported by the college officials, accusing Gibson's Bakery of racism. It shows how a social and political climate can trigger actions against businesses, regardless of their size and reputation, and especially when things are taken out of context and misrepresented.

For this reason, it is important to paint the public picture ahead of time and to be ready for any possible situations that could lead to litigation. Obviously, we need to condemn any form of discrimination and create a culture within the company that does not support such behavior. We need to have clear standards and make sure we adhere to them to be able to counter all accusations, especially those aimed at ruining the company's reputation.

We cannot prepare for every possible eventuality, but we can establish good working practices and build credibility and reputation by following the regulations as well as conducting our business thoughtfully and conscientiously within the prevalent social consensus.

We should also be aware of the opportunities for individuals to weaponize media and social networks to discredit companies in pursuit of fame or financial gain. We need to make sure

---

21. https://www.nytimes.com/2022/09/08/us/oberlin-bakery-lawsuit.html

we have a good reputation, setting standards in line with regulations, building trust and rapport with the public, and making continual efforts toward maintaining it, which helps us alleviate any potential damage inflicted by future incidents. We need to be able to show a continuum of excellence with the above-mentioned elements in order to defend our reputation, as trying to build one once accused of wrongdoing will be extremely hard. This is due to the lack of focus and the public's desire to analyze content. Public opinion is mainly formed by the headlines, and most people do not investigate much further or deeper to understand the circumstances. This is due to a shortened attention span caused by technological and social media information overload. Most of the information is irrelevant, but it is there and processed by our brains, which leaves little time to focus and actually invest in understanding or coming to an informed conclusion based on the facts. It appears as if this phenomenon has conditioned most people to "outsource" their logic to trusted authorities and so adopt the opinions of such authorities without scrutiny. They let the "experts" decide for them as it is more convenient, and it provides an opportunity to distance themselves from responsibility for their actions in case of failure. This is why we need to have enough of a history of excellence with an established culture and high standards within the company to be able to immediately give the public enough appealing information to grab their attention and refute accusations within that short attention span. Perhaps it sounds crazy, but it is just the reality of the time we live in, and we need to think of the best possible situations and the best approach to resolving those. This will become an important part of the company, and it should get the required attention and investment to be able to fulfill its role. We should not have the mentality that this cannot happen to us, as we could very well have a disgruntled employee or unsatisfied customer attempting to discredit the company and distort or ruin our public image.

3.4 Sales and marketing

This is part of each and every business, regardless of the industry, and it is deeply interconnected with communicating with the public. Each company is trying to sell either products, services, or ideas to make a profit and fulfill its purpose. Each company is trying to reach and grab the attention of potential customers/clients and persuade them to invest in their products or services. There are various ways this can be achieved, especially in this age of technology. The important thing to remember is to be truthful and honest in the presentation of the product/service, which doesn't seem to be the case in most instances.

Misleading consumers seems to be a widespread occurrence, as we have already mentioned, with examples from the pharmaceutical and automobile industries.

Why is this the case? We need to look deeper into the company's mission and vision, along with the standard and compliance, to detect misleading practices that might have evaded our processes and established as a norm in fulfilling the financial target regardless of the impact on our company and society.

We can find several reasons behind it:

1. This might be due to greed or the inability to develop original and plausible solutions by the team of people in charge of marketing and sales.

2. It could be that the marketing and sales team is tasked to compensate for the product or service shortcomings.

3. Great social, political, or legislative pressure to align with the new standard.

We then need to address that and see which steps need to be taken to rectify it and prevent it from impacting our company and causing a detrimental blow to its reputation.

We also need to be honest and recognize market shifts and new legislations that might make our market position harder, with a tight time frame to adjust and deliver results.

If we let this go and turn a blind eye, we are running a risk of setting a precedent and diverting our company away from ingenuity and excellence toward opportunism and fraudulent practices, which will hurt our company in the long run.

We can look at Meta and notice a 180-degree shift in paradigm concerning their sales and marketing pitch in 2025, with the Covid pandemic aftermath and new political powers emerging in the US.[22] The new approach to censorship and free speech aligns with the "Community Notes model" of competitive company X, formerly known as Twitter, and it indicates the adoption of a process aligned with the competitor, who happens to be in line with the new administration. Meta introduced another change of policy with DEI (diversity, equity, and inclusion) after the same was introduced by other companies, as reported by CBS News and Fox Business on January 10th, 2025.[23] [24] This also aligns with the new political direction as

---

22. https://about.fb.com/news/2025/01/
meta-more-speech-fewer-mistakes/

23. https://www.cbsnews.com/news/
meta-dei-programs-mcdonalds-walmart-ford-diversity/

24. https://www.foxbusiness.com/politics/meta-policy-chief-says-
decision-end-dei-ensures-company-hires-the-most-talented-people

they have introduced a new bill governing DEI - "Dismantle DEI Act of 2024."[25]

These shifts will have both positive and negative impacts on the company:

1. Some supporters will penalize the shift of direction, considering it to be far out of their social norms and political views.

2. Others might reward their trust as the company has now come closer to their political views and social norms.

3. There will also be others who will take it with a "pinch of salt," reserving their trust while expecting another shift of marketing and sales under immense social and political influences in the future.

In any case, their supporters and critics will want to know why. And most importantly, why now?

Everyone will form their opinions based on their political and social norms, but the big influence will come from the predominant media leaders and political supporters in helping paint a public picture of integrity and interest in the greater good.

We have mentioned this paradigm in our first chapter, as all great social shifts are fueled by immense media and political support and pressure, and we would be naïve to think this will not be the case now.

The future will show if this shift was a good marketing and sales strategy.

---

25. https://www.congress.gov/bill/118th-congress/senate-bill/4516/text

CHAPTER 4

Creating the standard

4.1 Creating training requirements

Identifying a mission and vision gives us the direction that frames factors and considerations. The legal framework, along with incorporated risk management, keeps us in line with the mission, vision, and applicable laws. Now, we are left with creating the standard. What does that mean? It means that we need to come up with individual and group tasks, respectively, depending on the line of business we are in, along with the optimal processes, procedures, and technology complementing our company's mission, if we are to deliver the best results. This helps us with setting and keeping the set standard while providing the best products or services.

This part is essential as it gives us the standard to adhere to and to scrutinize against. There are several steps to this process:

1. We are going to determine key aspects of our product/ service production, selling, and delivery, with complementing processes, procedures, and technology.

2. We will then analyze and determine the group tasks that need to be completed by a team that is adhering to the same standard.

3. Then we will need to look into individual skills and trainings that are essential to complete all the required group tasks.

At the end of this process, we will be left with a clear understanding of the required tasks for each position, as well as the personal skills required for the same. All of this will depend on the type of business and will need to be tailored for each market and product. This is an ongoing process that requires continual monitoring and flexibility as the circumstances keep changing.

We need to be mindful that more is not always better. Meaning we should tailor our training requirements to fit our purpose by bringing our employees to the required standard and equipping them to successfully execute required tasks at the most satisfying level. There is nothing worse than wasting everyone's time by implementing unnecessary training that does not contribute to the above.

If we overwhelm our employees with extraneous training that does not enhance their performance and does not give them opportunities to grow and develop, then we will negatively influence them in different ways:

1. They may become uninterested in future development and training opportunities, which will then result in push-back.

2. They can also become frustrated and develop feelings of unworthiness if they are being brainwashed by the company. Especially once the company decides to introduce specific training aimed at human behavior in an attempt to change the social consensus to fit within the company's targeted social behavior.

We can see that "political correctness" has been creeping into every aspect of our lives along with the "green" agenda. Nothing wrong with new ideas and striving to make changes for the better, but doing so without taking into consideration the negative aspects of the same will not produce desirable results.

We have ample examples in history where theoretical ideas, once implemented, have turned into a devastating system that negatively affected generations of people, caused by blind obedience resulting in a group reluctance to question the agenda.

It seems it is the larger companies that have set the new goal of re-educating people to fit their projected political or social goals. This means that they are molding their employees to behave and think in certain ways contrary to those employees' personal beliefs while simultaneously projecting a company image that celebrates diversity and inclusion. Diversity and inclusion, along with "green" and "Sustainable", are new "get out of jail" cards for companies as they hide behind those words while continuing the same, sometimes corrupt, practices wrapped in big words without true meaning.

This practice is concerning as the leaders implementing them are being molded within or hired based on their matching political and social beliefs and not necessarily on their competence. This then concentrates forces, with unified beliefs, within the decision-making and influential heart of the leadership, creating an exclusive and divisive society not able to accept diversity nor include anyone not sharing the same beliefs. Scary, as those are the same practices, although achieved through force, by totalitarian societies in not-so-distant history. The same can only lead to a slow and painful degradation of those companies and, subsequently, of society itself.

This is why we need to focus on competency, excellence, ingenuity, and innovation, regardless of the personal belief systems of the employees or of society. We need to respect and cherish diversity of beliefs and cultures, but this should not influence or drive our decisions. The best person for a certain job should get the job based on their skill set and knowledge, and those need to be demonstrated rather than belief systems or political sympathies.

4.2 Training and Certification

We need to keep a close eye on industry standards and those certifications required for our employees, in addition to our company training programs. We must also identify new opportunities and create our own certifications of competence to maintain our focus on excellence. Notwithstanding all this, we should beware of falling down a rabbit hole. We should not adopt the mindset of "just in case." Our focus should be on essential training and certification, not on piling them up because we have a "the more, the better" mentality. It is counterproductive to have an employee go through elaborate brainwashing processes with numerous certifications, the majority of which are not needed for the job. This would water down the whole process and divert attention from our set goals, which provide an opportunity for self-development and growth.

This must be accorded the very highest priority and requires the right people for the job: staff who understand the mission, legal framework, and desired standards directing the tailored training and certification for each job. Unfortunately, it seems to be a widespread occurrence to have incompetent people in charge of this most responsible and crucial part of the operation, as if underperformance is a required skill for the job, which brings us to the saying: "Those who can, do; and those who can't, teach."

It is imperative to get this right; otherwise, we are at risk of not setting competency, excellence, ingenuity, and innovation as our foundations and core values. Sitting in a lecture that has no benefit, especially if the same is delivered by individuals not experts in the subject matter, will produce negative results.

Developing the training and certification standards cannot be done by individuals who do not understand the complexity of the jobs, along with the challenges and limitations encountered while performing it. This means that input from employees is essential in creating comprehensive and tailored training, which brings everyone to the same standard. It should be tailored to reflect not only the peaks of the job but also all the downsides. It is counterproductive to paint a wrong picture to employees during the initial or on-the-job training, which contradicts reality solely as a rubber stamp. That is an absolute waste of time and effort, with negative results killing our employees' trust and enthusiasm.

Well-tailored training/certification aimed specifically at increasing competency and performance as a result of self-development and growth brings a high level of appreciation and purpose to the minds of employees. It makes them feel appreciated and important because the company has made an effort to invest in their personal development and growth. This then results in enthusiastic engagement and the implementation of newly developed skills by the employees. It also empowers them to speak out and suggest improvements, which will then benefit the operation and help identify new procedures, along with training opportunities. Additionally, they will take ownership of the adopted standards and serve as advocates for the same among other employees.

We might find ourselves in a situation where numerous certifications are required, as mandated by the respective governing bodies. This is something that is unavoidable, but it needs to be made smooth and practical for our employees so they accept the requirements, even if the applicability of such qualifications is not immediately obvious to them.

We should not forget that our employees, although they might hold the lowest positions within the company, often understand the challenges experienced in the execution of the operation, which may be invisible to the governing bodies and their certification developers. In other words, the workers may have a better idea about what is wrong and the solutions than the government agency employee developing training certification requirements, which is usually done as a reaction to a certain catastrophe or near one.

4.3 Introducing new protocols and procedures

This might be necessary due to various reasons, which include changes in regulations, system changes, and market fluctuations, perhaps as a reaction to an incident.

Before we go down the road of introducing new protocols and procedures, we need to ask ourselves:

1. Is that the best course of action?

2. Is it necessary?

3. Is it going to increase productivity or just become another nuisance for the employees?

Ticking a box is not a smart strategy, and it is the first sign of incompetence within the responsible leadership. This is why this step should be undertaken once all the brainstorming opportunities have been exhausted, which includes important input from employees, especially those who are specialists in particular segments of the operation.

If we are reacting to the change in regulations, we need to look into current protocols and procedures with complementing training and certifications to identify opportunities to adjust them accordingly and to avoid adding unnecessary additional training.

We need to be ready to adjust at any time, and we can only do that if we have employed highly qualified and enthusiastic individuals who are communicating in a timely and accurate manner. We need to make sure that there is no tendency to get attached to existing training and consider them their "babies" by the persons developing them. This poses a potential challenge since individuals might find themselves offended and reluctant to change or replace the training they developed, either fully or in part. So, they keep their "baby" and refuse to get in line with the necessary changes. If this goes under the radar, we are at risk of failing in our set mission goals and diverting from the path of excellence.

As for the system change, we need to look into the new system requirements and whether the new system is similar to the old one and, if so, in which segments. We need to get all users adequately trained with the possibility of selected employees obtaining the "Train the trainer" certifications, if available.

Also, is it plausible to have all training covered by the system developers and have them deliver the required training to have the necessary certification? This might be in-person training or perhaps an online session, as applicable.

This is a good approach for several reasons:

1. The developers have in-depth knowledge of the system and all its abilities along with its limitations, so they can relay those better to the final user. They can also

answer all the questions during the Q&A sessions and we, the audience, can even help them discover new opportunities to tailor the systems for the end user.

2. Taking a step back and having a third party deliver training and issue the certification minimizes our responsibility, in case of user error resulting in a potential lawsuit.

3. It also keeps the costs down in case flexibility and adjustment are required regularly.

Market fluctuations might raise red flags and have a lot of leaders on their toes and hyperventilating. This might trigger a case of self-importance in some of them and have them demanding changes at short notice. The same should be looked at from a short- and long-term perspective. Is this a short-term market fluctuation, or is this a tectonic shift in the market that requires deep changes in our approach?

Obviously, the above will also depend on the type of business we are in and the nature of the market or operational shift. Changes in raw material supply in production are likely to have a greater impact than changes in procedural methods in the service industry.

A short-term shift should be analyzed and its cause identified to be able to determine which procedural or training changes are required, if any. Perhaps an adjustment in procedures and training frequency could compensate for the identified gap and help with the short-term adjustment.

A long-term shift, or a permanent one, requires a different approach and probably the involvement of the risk management and legal departments to determine the right approach in tailoring procedures and training for the new operational requirements while preventing over-exhausting the employees and creating fatigue.

Reaction to an incident should be proportional and not overdone. This means we should avoid going into "flight mode" and trying to put a blanket over every possibility of an error. We need to first analyze the incident and detect the cause based on the facts and not opinions. We then need to understand how it could have been avoided. Is it a human error? Process flaw? Equipment failure? Or perhaps a combination of elements? We then look into the existing protocols and procedures to detect the opportunity for improvement without going into the unnecessary process of introducing new protocols and procedures, with, subsequently, new training, which could further complicate existing processes without elevating the safety aspect and even potentially making it less safe. So, we need to remain calm and rational when analyzing and deciding on the right approach.

We need to identify the need for new protocols, procedures, and training and set on the right path to providing a comprehensive set of training courses absolutely necessary to complement the company expectations and establish a working culture within the company.

The risk of overdoing it starts the moment we have a set team of people becoming comfortable in their roles. Every person in every society is looking for the purpose and the meaning, which then gets embedded in their character and personality. This is why people cling to the jobs and organizations that they are comfortable with, defending the same from the outside elements, which might be negative, but also positive but perceived as negative, due to a lack of flexibility combined with the fear of change. We have all heard the expression: "We have always done it this way." This then becomes dangerous territory as the training and certification team becomes self-focused and not focused on the mission. Remember, we strive for excellence, ingenuity, and innovation.

This is why we need to be realistic and keep ourselves in the present while monitoring future trends. We should avoid getting paranoid or overly concerned but should set a standard for detecting and monitoring the risks involved in our operation. This is done in several ways:

1. Come up with a risk assessment and, if applicable, threat assessment.

2. Develop comprehensive, but intuitive, forms for the evaluation of the risk/threat assessment, as applicable.

3. Set the required periodical assessments commenced by the trained individuals, while creating simple forms of detection/reporting, for the rest of the employees who will expect to be exposed to the indicators of the risk/threat elevation.

4. Provide necessary training to all employees, along with access to the risk/threat detection recording platform, to identify the shift of the risk/threat level in a timely manner.

By doing this, we create a society of focused and switched-on individuals monitoring the set standard and empowered to participate in problem detection and resolution. It gives a sense of importance, involvement, and ownership, along with the satisfaction of being important and contributing. This then results in everyone monitoring the operation and being actively engaged in maintaining the safest routes toward the set company goal. We achieve more by accepting differences and a variety of personal beliefs and by setting the expectation of working toward the same goals through competence, as our employees are happy to participate when they feel part of the team, qualified, and empowered to contribute. This approach minimizes the possibility of complacency, resulting in a disregard for positive inputs.

4.4 Introduction of the new equipment

Do we need it? That is the question we need to ask ourselves. And if so, why do we need it? Obviously, technology is good, and, in most cases, it adds to the process and makes it more efficient. However, we can go down the road of relying only on technology.

We should also understand who is proposing new technology and why. Have we weighed all its benefits and limitations? Has the same been introduced to our competition, and what is the feedback? We should be open to new technology, but obviously only if it complements our mission and makes the operation smoother and more efficient.

This is something that is also expense-dependent. In most of the big companies, such investment is going to be looked at by various departments, including financial and legal. Why? Because cost efficiency is the primary goal of the companies which are run by and for profit. The decision is going to be made based on the calculation between the cost of the investment and the financial net benefit of the same. Unfortunately, it is pure numbers in most cases, and no other benefit is phased in, including the benefit for the employees.

The sad truth is that companies will do their best to avoid investment if not obliged to do so by regulation if the risk associated is far smaller than the benefit. This means they will calculate the potential financial risk of not having the said equipment and compare it with the cost of the equipment over a certain period of time. This simple math does not take into account humans and their well-being. This is one of the reasons most Western companies have chosen the East for their cheaper labor costs and loose regulations covering the well-being of the employees.

Sometimes, this practice is not so bad, as it pushes employees and leaders to think outside the box and come up with other solutions, which could bounce back to an organizational or training reorganization to adjust for the lack of equipment. On the other hand, this could also lead to a negative image portrayed toward the public and employees, resulting in a deflation of trust in the company. There is great danger in having a disgruntled employee as negativity and dissatisfaction can spread like wildfire, similar to panic in emergency situations.

So, needs must be communicated in the right manner to responsible decision-makers. This falls on the leaders responsible, who need to come up with concise data showing the need for the equipment in question, along with the benefits and positive operational impact it will have on the company's bottom line, compared to the risk of not introducing that equipment.

Sometimes, we will face individuals in a leader's role who come from a certain background, which perhaps gave them more decision-making power and independence, resulting in their inability to communicate in concise and persuasive ways to upper management.

This then results in a couple of dangerous outcomes:

1. The said leader is then left frustrated as upper management hasn't agreed to the proposal; so, the frustration might be passed on to the team if the leader does not exercise discretion when communicating with the team.

2. It might create a gap between upper management and the leader responsible, as the feeling of not being taken seriously might prevail. This might prevent future engagements, from the leader, in anticipation of a negative response.

3. Employees might lose trust in the leader as they might believe not enough effort was made, or no actions have been taken at all.

The result is obviously not laudable for various reasons, as it might widen the gap between the departments, reflecting negatively on the company's mission. It is imperative to have leaders empowered to speak up, but also to have the right person for the right position, based only on the required skill set for that position. Also, upper management should detect the lack of concise and discreet communication in order to address it, thereby providing honest feedback and helping the leader to enhance their communication skills.

We can have the opposite situation where a leader might have success in implementing new equipment, which does not improve the operation but rather imposes a greater workload on employees and even exposes them to scrutiny in case of failure.

This might result in several unwanted outcomes:

1. The leader is perceived as not involved and not interested in employee feedback, further widening the gap between the leader and the employees. This is a dangerous situation as it results in a tectonic shift of trust, which is the vital foundation of every operation.

2. The employees have increased stress levels and are reluctant to utilize the imposed equipment, resulting in a deflation of performance.

3. The above could become acute and the same could

reflect on team performance, while grabbing the attention of upper management. It could result in deeper analysis and involvement of upper management, which could put the leader responsible in a position where their actions will need to be explained.

The risk of the above scenario is having the leader responsible close in and become uninterested in the future improvement of the operation, along with distancing from the upper management. This is devastating for the operation as communication will cease, and improperly filtered information will be passed from the leader responsible to the upper management, thereby preventing relevant and potentially important scrutiny.

Both examples show how critical is the communication and the acceptance of competency as the main characteristic for all our employees. We need to be conscious of the negative effect of miscommunication, along with sending a wrong message by not communicating the reasons for not accepting proposals from our employees. Saying no is not the problem, but rather how we say it. We can reject proposals and leave the employee contemptuous of the outcome and reluctant to step forward with new proposals in the future. The employee's disappointment and reluctance to participate in the future will cause a loss of incentive and initiative.

We also need to make sure the new equipment proposal is not compensation for a flawed process, inadequate training, or a substitution for proper engagement by the employees. Equipment is supposed to boost and complement the performance of employees while increasing productivity and supporting the company's mission.

Once the new equipment is acquired and implemented, we need to determine the need for proper training in utilizing it. Perhaps the new equipment is an updated version of the old, so no extensive training is required, and quick on-the-job training can be delivered by technicians. However, if the acquired equipment is new to the company, it will require additional training for all users, which can be obtained in one of two ways:

1. Sending employees to the manufacturers' training facilities for basic, advanced, or train-the-trainer courses, as appropriate.

2. Attendance of the manufacturer's trainers at the company facility to provide basic, advanced, or train-the-trainer course, as appropriate.

The decision is going to depend on the cost associated with each approach. Either way, the cost-effective approach is to select employees for the train-the-trainer course and get them certified in training the rest of the employees. This leaves us more flexibility with training schedules and empowers employees to embrace the equipment and empower other employees to do the same. It also helps minimize the cost associated with training all required employees. The risk of doing so comes with the possibility of a flawed training delivery if the selected employees completing the train-the-trainer course do not possess the adequate technical abilities to comprehend all the technical specifics of the equipment or have a limited ability to convey that information to the rest of the employees.

ZORAN VIDOVIĆ

CHAPTER 5
Establishing the compliance process

O nce we have established the training and certification requirements complemented by the optimal technology, systems, and processes supporting the set standard, we need to look into a mechanism for maintaining that standard.

We will need to establish compliance processes and responsible people trained to execute them. This should not be a case of ticking the box but rather an opportunity to get an in-depth insight into the true status of our standard, including the knowledge, equipment, procedures, and processes. So, we need to make sure the process is not tailored to bring an apparently desired result and have everyone content with the perception of perfection while making sure they do not step on anyone's toes. It is imperative that the compliance section of the company does not come under the same management it is supposed to be auditing, as we run a risk of diluting the findings and turning a "blind eye."

Compliance is a very "lonely" job and does not allow many bonding opportunities for the employees in charge, as they will be perceived as the "secret police" within the company. This can, and needs to be, prevented by making the process clear and transparent with the right people employed for the job.

This is crucial for multiple reasons:

1. One is to prevent the power-driven individual from executing such a responsible job, from distorting re-

sults, driven by an interest in self-glory at the expense of the subject employees. We do not want the compliance team to become a source of frustration and stress, but rather to be perceived as a helpful team focused on boosting excellence.

2. There is also a risk of having employees distort and hide the facts to prevent being called out and put at risk of losing their jobs. This is hard to avoid, even with the best intentions, as it is a natural reaction of most individuals to try to present themselves in the best possible light when confronted by authority.

One way of avoiding the above is to recruit an approachable compliance team with good communication skills who clearly convey the process and the intent to the employees during the conduct of the audit. There will be some adjustment time until this is achieved, as the employees will need to be convinced of the positive approach, even when improvement opportunities have been detected during the compliance audits. When this is achieved, trust is built between the compliance team and the employees, and it will be passed on, in due course, to new employees, helping to build a sustained good working atmosphere fueled by trust and common goals.

We need to understand the mindset of the crowd. We identify with people in the same situation and can easily adopt the behavior displayed by others within the crowd, especially when confronted by an authority perceived as insensitive and not trustworthy. Trust is imperative in this critical dynamic of the company. We cannot emphasize that enough to the whole team, and we need to make sure the same is set as a core value in the compliance unit.

They need to understand that the company's mission is the goal and not personal success. It is not their personal "success" in detecting anomalies and non-compliance that matters. It is the set tone of the process and success in establishing trust and an environment where employees volunteer information and detect flaws in operations and established processes. So, success is measured by the detected opportunities for growth, and the same should be communicated clearly to all employees.

Compliance processes should be readily available for everyone to understand, and clear feedback should be provided to all participants. It should be considered a reflection of the current status and as a tool for growth through improvement.

We need to allow for discussion and two-way communication to understand the reason behind the detected opportunities for improvement. It should not serve as a platform and leverage for punishing employees but as a tool for detecting deviations from the set standard and opportunities for improvement and growth.

Having employees from varying levels and disciplines engaged in the compliance process, especially at the management level, could be the way to establish trust. We might have some temporary compliance positions or the possibility for various employees to participate after undergoing training and qualification. This might ease the resistance of employees and leadership and prevent the possibility of the team becoming an "island" on their own within the company. We do not want a group of people feeling untouchable and powerful as this creates a coherent group of "exclusive" members gradually growing in self-importance and considering themselves unmatchable. This is a real danger, and the same might be identified and used for personal goals of equally self-focused upper management leaders, creating good grounds for kickback reactions.

5.1 Record-keeping

We need to secure a way of having permanent and unmanipulated records detailing adherence to the set standard. This is essential for several reasons:

1. It gives us insight into the current status of equipment, processes, procedures, meeting the company's standard, and the training for each employee with outstanding and due, or possibly overdue, training.

2. It serves as a record in a case of legal dispute regardless of whether it's between the employee and the company or a third party.

3. It serves as auditable proof of competency and adherence to the required regulations set by the governing bodies responsible.

So, record-keeping is very important and a critical part of the compliance process. To avoid being taken lightly, auditing is necessary, along with effective feedback, to establish our professional culture.

The importance of maintaining the integrity of the process needs to be clearly communicated to all involved. The process needs to be transparent and protected from any possibility of abuse and manipulation, especially from unauthorized changes or data falsification for personal gain.

Compliance and risk management set and maintain the direction of a company toward success. It is important to understand this and set up these two departments in a complementary relationship, allowing for the identification of new opportunities and the detection of any elements preventing us from maximizing profitable outcomes.

CHAPTER 6
Hiring requirements

6.1 Defining the hiring process

If we did a good job in all areas, as detailed in previous chapters, the hiring process solves itself. The company's mission and vision dictate the direction, further dissected by the business legal framework, standard, training, and compliance process. This leaves us with a set list of skills needed to fulfill each role in the company, along with the set standards and complementing job descriptions that need to be adhered to maintain excellence.

This segment, although it might be perceived as secondary, is extremely important as it will bring to the table the new workforce that complements the company's mission and vision. We then work toward excellence and ingenuity, as the core of our company is our employees, who have been chosen for their competencies and skills.

As in all previous segments, the hiring process needs to be established to support the company's mission and vision and establish expectations of competency, innovation, excellence, and ingenuity, central to our company values leading to success. This segment will be developed alongside the legal and compliance sections, along with department leadership, to set the standard, which will underline the hiring process along with the hiring agent's skills to be able to produce the required results.

The most important will be the input from department leadership and their surveys, conducted within each department, to reflect the standards achieved and practices implemented by the employees performing the job. This part is crucial but highly sensitive. We can find ourselves falling down the abyss of distorted personal opinions if the pool of people providing feedback is not at the required standard due to poor compliance processes or leadership styles. So, this is a closed loop, sensitive, and fragile, as the result depends on the performance of all segments.

Setting this from the get-go is much easier than trying to fix it once the company is established and up and running. Fixing it would require support and cooperation from all segments, even those that are the root cause of the problem.

Either way, we will face a list of opinions and practices, most of them contradicting each other, as the employees and the leaders all have different personalities with various previous experiences and backgrounds. We will get opposing positions on important matters and will need to determine which one brings us closer to the company's mission. We will then adopt it and maintain a professional culture where input and suggestions are treasured and encouraged to receive feedback from the employees. We should strive to implement change from the ground up and not necessarily the other way around.

The hiring process consists of several elements:

1. Candidates' specifics:
   a) Job description
   b) Required skills
   c) Education and certification
   d) Experience in similar roles

2. Selection process:

   a) Cover letter and CV analysis

   b) Interview process

   c) Testing process, as applicable (job specific)

   d) Medical exam, as applicable

3. Hiring:

   a) Offering the job, detailing salary and other perks

   b) Welcome package with additional information

   c) Expectations set with the stated probation period

We can outsource this process to specialized companies, but we need to make sure our company's mission and standards are clearly communicated, along with set expectations to prevent them from being lost in translation, ensuring we do not compromise on the essentials.

We need to be mindful that we will potentially limit our abilities to identify suitable candidates when outsourcing this segment, especially when computer programs are utilized to select the prime candidates from a great number of applicants.

A personal approach should be used, when feasible, to minimize the possibility of missing potential candidates due to CVs or cover letters that sit outside the usual. Obviously, our candidates should make an effort to present themselves adequately, but sometimes an unforgiving and rigid approach could lead us to hire boosted and "facelifted" CVs with qualities not matched by the presented candidate. We should insist on the contents and not necessarily the form.

The hiring process should not be a one-stop shop, as the specifics of the potential candidates, once narrowed down by the hiring agents, should be presented to the leaders responsible for review and additional comments to assist in choosing the best applicant.

We should refrain from requiring unnecessary details not pertaining to the advertised position, such as sex and appearance, as applicable. Obviously, this might not be possible if such characteristics are pertinent to the posted position.

6.2 Hiring agent's skill set

The hiring agents need to have in-depth knowledge of the positions they are hiring for, which is a highly challenging task as it is impossible to have limited hiring agents exposed to all the jobs. So, communication and surveys are key to obtaining important information and allowing the formalization of expectations for each position, which can then be clearly communicated to potential employees by our hiring agents.

Hiring agents should be aware of our company's mission, as well as the position our company is striving for, within the context of the selected market. This is essential to be able to understand the strengths we are striving for, which some candidates might possess but have not pushed in their focus.

Hiring agents need to be skilled and able to read through the façade to uncover any hidden character lines among applying candidates. This is not so easy to achieve for a person not emotionally connected with the company, especially if the person is not experienced enough nor has been exposed to employment or experiences allowing personal development and growth in the relevant field. Does it mean we cannot employ a young person as a hiring agent? No, but it does suggest those employees should be trained and mentored by individuals with the required background, experience, and skill set to set the person on a path to success, resulting in a performance complementing the company's goals.

In this job, it is also crucial to be left untainted by political and social shifts, as the same might negatively influence the hiring process and shift the focus from important and measurable elements toward personal prejudices. We do not want the hiring agents to be impressed by the candidate's personal beliefs or political stance, which could influence their decision. The only measure should be competency.

6.3   Required skill set for the candidates

This needs to be identified before the hiring process commences. We need to have a clear understanding of the skill sets we seek in our employees for each position based on the job descriptions and tasks required to be performed. It will also depend on the working conditions as some locations might require more specific skill sets and performance abilities than others.

Job descriptions should be included in each job's advertisement, and we should be careful of overcomplicating it and making it sound like a job only a few can get. Making a job sound overly complicated, requiring an extraordinary skill set, which in reality is not crucial, will cost us suitable candidates. This approach can have negative impacts:

1.   It will discourage potential candidates from applying as they might not believe their skill set and experience match the requirement.

2.   It might encourage some candidates to boost their CV or cover letter to get the required attention which can backfire later during the interview and background check.

3. It might even push qualified candidates away if they understand a position's requirements and know the expectation does not reflect reality. This then makes us look fraudulent, misleading and dishonest.

Remember, we are looking for the right candidate for the right job, and we strive to attract the best possible candidates possessing all the required skills and experience. It is in our best interest to tailor this process to attract the right candidates to minimize the time and financial resources spent on it.

We need to understand that everyone is playing a game here. The companies are looking for the best employee, hopefully at the lowest possible price, and the employees are looking for the best employer, hoping for the highest possible salary.

Depending on the position, the tone for the above could be set by the company or by the potential candidates. It all depends on supply and demand. Companies can have different approaches depending on employee supply and demand:

1. High demand but a short supply of skilled employees will require a company to offer better salary packages along with other perks to attract potential candidates. They will also need to tailor job advertisements to capture a broader audience and ensure a bigger pool of candidates to choose from. The company will need to invest in considering less experienced or inexperienced candidates to satisfy the need.

2. High demand and high supply will have a similar effect with not necessarily a need to adjust the job ad to capture a broader audience, nor to necessarily consider inexperienced candidates. They will compete with salary and perks packages, but will need to stay within the marked trends, adjusting to employee expectations, to prevent a quick turnaround of employees.

3. Low demand and low supply are tricky since this allows for little or no wiggle room. It means that there are scarce numbers of potential candidates with the required skill sets and experience, probably due to low demand. It will affect the company, forcing it to compromise in two ways:

   a. Lower the standard to capture the potential candidates from a pool of candidates possessing somewhat different skills and experience, which could be elevated to match requirements.

   b. Look at the existing employees possessing similar skill sets and experience, which can be elevated to match requirements. Then hire new employees for that role instead.

4. Low demand and high supply. This is a company's heaven. The company can make the rules and have the candidates lower their expectations in hope of employment. This provides the company with a pool of skilled and experienced candidates to choose from, while setting the highest expectations. We just need to be aware of the demand and supply ratio change in the future to adjust compensation packages and prevent the turnaround of employees.

The bottom line is we need to be realistic when advertising a job position to attract the right candidates and make the hiring process as smooth and as quick as possible while minimizing the risk of expensive employee turnover.

6.4 Succession planning

This is imperative! This puts us in a leading position, especially during periods of high demand and short supply. Obviously, we prefer to keep existing employees and should create working conditions, along with suitable compensation packages appealing to the employees so they stay loyal to us and strive for development and growth within the company.

Unfortunately, there are other elements that influence employee rotation, such as personal reasons, no room for advancement, along with cutbacks during a recession, or special circumstances such as the COVID-19 pandemic. Although we would prefer to keep all our employees, circumstances such as the COVID-19 lockdowns and restrictions forced companies to take drastic measures and release some employees due to an inability to operate. This was, for instance, the case with the aviation and cruise industries. Due to flight and cruise restrictions, companies were not allowed to operate indefinitely, so they had to cut expenses to prevent bankruptcy. This resulted in their allowing a great number of employees to return to the employment market and subsequently find different opportunities. In doing so, those companies have lost valuable employees and, along with them, a know-how that took years to build. The wise approach would have been to keep essential personnel, which hopefully included employees with desired qualifications and great performance records.

To prevent losing a quality employee force, especially during normal operations, succession planning is essential and needs to be taken seriously. It should be designed with plans for advancing skilled individuals to higher positions when opportunities arise. The process should be designed to rely on measurable data collected by the performance and compliance systems, which support recommendations for promotion as advised by first-line leaders. This process needs to prevent advancing "favorite" candidates over the most qualified candidates to prevent creating a "trading" culture within the company. This process needs to communicate clearly the set expectations to all employees and provide adequate feedback. Employees considered for advancement need to be advised on their performance and current status, along with clear and measurable recommendations for improvement. This means they should be advised on progressing their performance, attitude, or behavior in a manner that supports the operation and the company's mission and not the preferred social standard set by the leader. We need to remember that we are looking for excellence and ingenuity and must not take into consideration personal preference and liking over measurable performance.

This process needs to be designed to prevent weaponization against certain employees by their leaders. This is achieved by setting clear rules and expectations for all leadership positions in the decision-making process, as this greatly affects employees' professional development and, subsequently, their lives.

It needs to be a highly monitored and controlled process with set evaluation protocols for each position, along with planned review, interview, and conversation intervals to preserve the integrity of the system. There need to be transparent promotion standards with current candidate lists based on set succession planning parameters. This will prevent any personal opinions from diluting the process for selected employees, as all the evaluation needs to be backed up by measurable elements as per the set matrix.

We need to be conscious of human nature, where personal interests might impede the required focus on the company's mission and the well-being of all the employees. Leaders should not be allowed to create their own little playground with personal rules as this negatively affects all employees and the company, especially in the long run.

CHAPTER 7
Performance feedback

7.1 Defining performance feedback frameworks

Performance feedback is natural and the basic approach to set expectations as well as advise employees of their current performance levels.

It is important that we set consistent standards and decide on the elements against which each employee's performance is going to be scrutinized.

Why so? For two reasons:

1. How can we hold someone accountable if we haven't set and clearly communicated the standard? Providing performance feedback gives us an opportunity to identify an employee's point of view and discuss limitations as perceived by the employer, while clearly articulating the company standard and expectations in a concise, understandable, and measured manner.

2. How can we hold someone accountable if we haven't advised them on their performance in timely manner? We cannot expect someone to identify their faults, as they might be performing to the best of their abilities under the impression that they are doing a great job. Perhaps they haven't been properly trained, which has reflected on their performance.

We need to determine which elements of overall performance are going to be isolated and focused on based on their impact on the company's goal. We will need to identify which individual or group tasks are crucial and need to be included in the process. This might be decided in conjunction with departmental expectations, or we can have an umbrella approach with uniform protocols for the whole company. Obviously, a tailored approach makes more sense, as not every position within the company requires the same skill set. It also provides concise information pertaining to the relevant job performance and avoids dubious segments that are not directly applicable to each position. This approach also makes the whole process meaningful and productive as the employees can relate to it and get valuable performance feedback with clear expectations for the direction of potential improvement. Obviously, there will be certain elements that apply to all employees regardless of job specifics.

The process needs to be considered highly sensitive and needs to be clearly set with explanations for both participants:

1. The leader providing feedback needs to understand which categories the feedback is referring to and how to evaluate the performance for each category. Also, the evaluation values need to be clearly explained, so the leader can easily decide on the appropriate value to attribute for each section.

2. The evaluation process needs to be explained to the employee and delivered in an understandable and concise manner.

7.2 Performance feedback form and process

The form should be intuitive and easily understandable to the employee and leader. Different categories should be clearly marked and divided for easy access and understanding. We need to make sure the same is a method for recordkeeping, and thus, recorded data cannot be manipulated after the event for compliance and succession planning purposes. If we are using an electronic system, which should be the preferred choice, it should record every entry with user ID information, date and time, and recorded feedback. Once saved, the system should not allow deletions, changes, or input but rather allow sequential updates by adding new inputs and marking them as additions to the previous one, with explanations. It also needs to allow for employee acknowledgment of the delivered feedback as a record of participation in the process, regardless of whether the conclusions are agreed or not, and with the outcome, as it does not serve as acceptance of the feedback and allows for further respectful dispute. This process should be clearly explained and governed by company policies, laying out how updates should be documented and in what circumstances. This process needs to be tightly monitored, and any violation sanctioned otherwise valuable information can be lost and manipulated to negatively reflect on the employees.

This process is a great tool that provides valuable feedback on the strengths and weaknesses of employees as well as the leaders. It helps to monitor and maintain a constant overview of employees while providing opportunities for the employees to elevate their performance and ask for additional training and direction. It also provides a clear overview of leaders' understanding and abilities to adhere to the set process.

7.3 Performance feedback delivery and expectations

Delivery should be done in private and not in a rush. We should underline all the good performances and highlight all the performances exceeding set expectations, along with all underperformances, giving a clear indication of what was not up to standard and how to elevate it. Feedback should be scheduled on a set rotation, which should be communicated to employees so they know when to expect it. It provides them with an opportunity to self-reflect and potentially elevate their performance without intervention due to heightened self-awareness guided by the pending performance review process.

The process should be an opportunity to have concise and constructive communication where both parties need to be honest and factual.

The evaluation feedback needs to be acknowledged by both parties, with the upper management's approval for any over and underperformance.

Also, we need to run a review and appeal process for employees disputing the evaluation.

The evaluation process should be designed to provide feedback on the employee's performance measured against the company's set standard for each evaluated category and, as such, present personal performance information. The information needs to be kept confidential, with access restricted to responsible decision-makers involved in the process. Employees should be allowed a copy of each evaluation with the ability to review their personal files.

This is essential for two reasons:

1. To maintain the integrity of the process. By providing written proof of the evaluation, we are backing our decision while providing an opportunity for the employee to reflect and take any action deemed necessary, including dispute. It allows minimum opportunity for misinterpretation as the evaluation is measurable and concise, based on the documented performance and the leader's interventions.

2. To prevent possible abuse of the process. Having a transparent and regulated evaluation process leaves little or no room for misinterpretations or unfairness as every segment of evaluation is regulated with a measurable performance grid.

The leader's role is to identify opportunities for improvement and to communicate the same to the employee in a timely manner and in easily understandable terms. Leaders also need to understand whether the feedback has been understood as intended and provide additional training and guidance as needed. All of this needs to be documented under relevant categories to maintain the integrity of the evaluation with a clear history of performance levels along with the leader's actions, including but not limited to training and certification, conversations, guidance, warnings, etc.

This is essential to prevent legal disputes with employees, as not everyone sees the same situation in the same manner. An employee dismissed from the company will surely have a different point of view than that of the leader responsible regarding the reasons for the separation. Sometimes, even the most comprehensive evaluation reports, with up-to-date employee files, are not enough for an employee to accept the facts. This is where attention to detail and adherence to company policies come into play, as the comprehensive evaluation reports and updated employee files serve as a record of employee performance. It also provides documentation supporting the leader's and company's actions and efforts to elevate performance to a satisfactory level while taking into consideration an employee's feedback and well-being.

7.4 Employee feedback

Employee feedback is essential in maintaining the integrity of the evaluation process along with the record keeping. We need to emphasize the importance of this segment as this is how we keep the process as close to flawless as possible. As mentioned earlier, employees and leaders will not always be on the same page and see reality from the same angle. It might not change the end result, but it serves as a good learning opportunity to understand different points of view and reasons for deviating from company expectations and standards. Perhaps there are logical and plausible explanations that cast light onto an opportunity for improvement within the evaluation process, hiring process, or even company policies and standards.

The opportunity to provide feedback and be listened to and acknowledged as a respected individual whose opinion is valuable will result in positive outcomes for all parties involved. It will make the employee feel respected and valued, even when separated from the company, as the process allows for feedback from and explanation by the employee. It also allows leaders to discover potential opportunities for improvement, which might result in relaxation or changes to the company standard based on repeated feedback from various employees. Perhaps a company's standard overshoots the performance capabilities of the selected cohort for the pertaining jobs.

Times are changing, and people are evolving, so companies need to stay in line with the changes while keeping focus on setting the path for success for both their employees and themselves.

This is achieved by listening, not by talking. Listen to current and former employees regardless of whether they have clear or twisted understandings of reality. If an employee is willing to speak up and express their opinion on the company's performance, we should embrace the feedback and analyze it to learn from it.

We should allow for anonymous feedback to capture as much information as possible from our employees.

This helps us in various ways:

1. The feedback could be concise and relevant, revealing flaws in procedures or established processes, including succession planning, performance feedback and compliance. This is pure gold as it comes from an employee point of view and there is a lot to be taken from it.

2. The feedback could very well be positive and emphasize the good organization and procedures within the company. It might show the direction we should continue with and reveal important elements for the employees.

3. It could also be incoherent and malicious without relevant information supporting the claim. There is also something to take out of this feedback too. Comparing received feedback with the recorded performance for the employee, if the employee is known, we can learn a lot and paint a picture of personal performance in relation to the expectations of the employee. If the employee is anonymous, then the feedback serves as

a reference to compare to other feedback referring to the same segments of the operation or company. This gradually builds up to a signal which might lead us toward the source of the frustration that might not be easy to discover otherwise, such as an established hostile climate within a certain department or a team.

4. Feedback also speaks volumes about the person providing it. It can tell us what the person is focusing on and what their priorities are. It can subsequently help us detect the characteristics that can help us tailor the job offerings, or perhaps the job requirements.

Sometimes, employees might perceive certain behaviors as hostile and, due to their character, they might decide they are unacceptable, although the reality might be to the contrary. So, the feedback presents an opportunity to discuss the differences and resolve them before they become issues.

We have all met the oddball individual who fails to integrate with the majority. This is not necessarily a bad thing as the person probably just lives in a slightly different reality than the rest of us, which often enables a superior performance in some respects. They might be more proficient in some skills that do not require communication and fitting within the group. We need to explore that and detect if the person is simply different with a lot to offer. We need to identify what this person is offering and work on it, obviously, so long as the person's behavior is not negatively affecting other employees, operations, or the company. Perhaps giving additional attention to that individual might encourage them to work harder on social aspects while excelling in their field of expertise under our guidance. So, we turn an oddball misfit, not accepted by others, into a respected, successful employee.

CHAPTER 8
Different leadership styles

8.1 What to strive for?

We are looking for an enthusiastic approach, along with compassion and the sensibility to connect with and understand people. Leaders should possess the ability to focus on what is important while being able to split focus and energy to achieve all the set goals by the set deadline. They should have the required skill set and confidence, preferably with complementary experience, to be able to understand job expectations and deliver results by setting excellence, ingenuity, and integrity as core values within the team, supported by open communication. Leaders should encourage growth and development in each member of the team, complemented by supporting procedures, processes, training, and equipment, which, together, drive results and success. They need to provide continued guidance and support to every team member, with concise and honest feedback directing the employees toward excellence. They should feel the beat of the team and react to the smallest change in the rhythm to prevent synergy loss while monitoring, assessing, and building a climate complementing the team's desired performance in delivering results in line with the company's mission.

8.2 "Red flags"

8.2.1 Withholding information

We need to stay alert for a tendency to withhold information, blocking the flow of ideas and stopping competent employees from expressing ideas and potential solutions.

Reasons for this can range from not understanding the information, withholding it to avoid responsibility, or perceiving it as a power and a leverage for domination. Withholding information is a form of dominance, especially over capable and competent employees who might be perceived as a potential threat.

This is not something reserved for the upper management; on the contrary, this must be the modus operandi for wannabe leaders on all levels. With this in mind, the upper management might be more susceptible to the "God complex."

This is important as it can destroy a good working environment in a short period of time. It can negatively influence even senior employees and lead them into a state of inferiority, questioning themselves. This then creates good grounds for division and inferiority to take over and establish itself.

Subsequently, it leads to the employment and promotion of people not striving for excellence and ingenuity, which slowly leads to a hostile working environment where everyone is focusing on themselves and not cooperating for multiple reasons:

1. Cooperation requires acceptance and partnering from all sides. We can have situations where an employee striving for excellence does not express opinions nor attempt to work as a team member due to fear of not being accepted, or perhaps even ridiculed by others

not striving for the same.

2. Requesting cooperation (due to not being able to perform a certain task), after which, on receiving positive results, the employee presents the work as their sole effort without recognizing the team's cooperation in order to advance their own self-promotion. This discourages any attempt at future cooperation as the outcome serves only selected individuals and not the team.

3. Being in the leader's ear, making sure to talk about everyone and report on everything for self-promotion purposes. It is quickly recognized by the team, resulting in a reduction or withdrawal of cooperation.

4. The leader downplaying and not recognizing an employee's good performance, instead going out of their way to recognize selected favorite employees, even when not deserved. This is to justify choices they have made and to advance their chosen subordinates.

All of the above create a climate preventing the growth of others focused on excellence and ingenuity. It creates an uncomfortable working environment with a clear message advancing favoritism as the main driver, irrespective of competence, pushing everyone to obey or resign.

It gradually removes opportunities for ingenuity and excellence as this approach relies on exploitation and not creation. It is like a parasite surviving by sucking on performance excellence until it's exhausted.

8.2.2 Power complex

We need to be aware of the danger of power syndromes developing within the company. This might be more predominant in lower management striving for advancement, although it could happen on every level. We should look for conflicting attitudes when observing relationships between subordinates and upper management, as they could reveal an unacceptable approach when addressing and dealing with subordinates. This approach prevents leaders from admitting mistakes, instead finding a person to blame, even when they are being escorted out of the company's door. It could render them unable to see reality due to a self-portrayed image of perfection and greatness. They might allow some employees to express ideas when in support of their causes, thereby increasing opportunities for self-promotion; however, they will not recognize nor reward the achievements of other individuals. They will create an expectation of the desired performance, which will be ignored as it will be deemed unworthy of recognition. No one will ever be good enough to be recognized and praised for a great job done due to the twisted image of the undisputed authority falsely promoting their own knowledge and abilities, casting shadows on everyone else, rendering them unworthy of recognition and praise.

Convictions, self-assurance, and confidence are welcome, but in combination with the ability for self-consciousness, self-reflection, and critique, which is not a virtue cherished by the leader adopting this unfortunate style of leadership. This approach could be manifested as looking for information that can be used against someone for selfish, personal benefit. It could also be manifested as seeking promotion into positions giving power over others with the ability to decide on other people's futures, with a tendency to be overly harsh in delivering negative feedback and subsequent evaluation and discipline.

It is a dangerous combination when a person adopting this style obtains power, as they will use it for their own benefit, regardless of the cost to others, while not allowing anyone else to express themselves and show their full potential. Obviously, it will take a while before this behavior is picked up and rectified by higher management, so it is important to entrench the company's culture, nurturing respect and honesty and empowering everyone to highlight undesirable behaviors without fear of repercussions.

8.2.3 Toxic behavior

Some people lacking sound leadership might succumb to a desire to divide and rule, resulting in unnecessary drama and conflict within the team. Such people are hard to work with and will not buy into the group cohesion that places the interests of the company first, as the urge to be the center of the universe is far greater than to become part of the team.

A leader adopting this style is deeply unhappy if not able to control the dynamic of the team. They will find a way to disturb the balance and disrupt cohesion within the team precisely because they are concerned and threatened by it. This approach will concentrate on detecting the weaknesses of each employee and using them to divide the team into groups to satisfy the need for control. They will then pick a temporary "favorite" employee to execute desired tasks, thus destroying what has become the fragile trust between the subordinate team members, promoting poor strategies and outcomes which will then be blamed on their least favorite employee(s) with the focus having shifted onto the construction of false narratives which will conclude with the punishment of easy targets who cannot defend themselves. This keeps everyone on their toes, with certain employees willing to obey (against their better judgment) in order to curry favor with the "ruler" and avoid becoming a target themselves as he searches for new victims. The motive is not necessarily striving for an upper leader position, as the main impulse to create division can be achieved within the team. They are usually/ always able to present themselves in a good light to upper management and establish trust by controlling the feedback to other leaders. It is surprising how many teams are affected by this, as it appears to be a widespread occurrence. Once confronted by a firm leader who does not fall for this kind of approach, they lay low and monitor the situation while gathering information that they might use against the leader or other coworkers respectively. It is imperative that leaders look for this kind of behavior and establish environments that do not support it: environments of transparency and trust, with incentives to speak the truth without repercussions.

We have mentioned some of the undesirable leadership styles that could be adopted by different types of leaders. There could also be a variety of different undesirable styles offering infinite combinations, but we have discussed a few that eliminate communication, cohesion, and ingenuity. The worst possible scenario is a combination of these mentioned styles, which presents a difficult obstacle in forming strong teams and achieving set goals in desired time frames. It is important to understand the difference between a leader's style and a type of leader (character and personality) as, although complementary, they are not necessarily the same. We might encounter specific leadership types fluctuating between leadership styles under various influences. This is why we may notice changes in leadership style. For some leaders under pressure imposed by the working environment or company's expectations, although once the pressure is removed, they usually revert to their default leadership style complementing their leadership type (character and personality). This could also result in a permanent change if the pressure continues, resulting in a change of the person's character and, subsequently, their leader type to accommodate for the desired leader style. This could be caused by a personal perception of the situation, the world, and reality, under imposed expectations conflicting with their personal character and beliefs.

Let's look further into basic elements of influencing leaders and shaping them into different leadership types while adopting specific leadership styles.

CHAPTER 9
Three basic types of Leaders

It is essentially impossible to capture every possible type of leader, as it depends on personal character and personality, influenced by built-in professional and personal experiences and motivation. However, we can draw parallels between various leader types and narrow them down to three basic types, portraying the whole spectrum from the best, the average, and the worst. We can then easily recognize shifts between these types and discover characteristics within every leader, shifting them between different leadership styles.

9.1 Leading by example, or the "follow me" leader

This type of leader has "us" and "we" in their dictionary and not "me," "myself," and "I." By doing so, this type of leader puts teamwork at the forefront and lets results speak for themselves. They understand that strength lies in the whole team, and the focus should be to strengthen the team by strengthening each person within. They make an effort to get to know the whole team as a unit and also each individual and focus on understanding their strengths and weaknesses. They will then focus on both and explore the weaknesses by strengthening them and empowering the employees to grow and develop while supporting further development of the strengths. They understand that each individual is different, and an individual approach will need to be taken to reach each member of the team to build trust and rapport. This leader will address each employee in a tailored manner to allow for personal character and will strengthen the individual on their journey to explore opportunities for improvement, development, and growth. They will address any concerns in a timely manner and directly with each member of the team in a truthful and factual manner. Also, team cohesion is imperative to deliver results, so any feedback from the team will be diverted to the respective departments for action. They will make sure to protect the team from any unwarranted implications raised by anyone by assessing the allegations and providing feedback as necessary.

It is hard to work with this leader for any individual lacking the desire to perform to the best of their abilities.

This type of leader is honest and direct in communication both with subordinates as well as upper management. Concise and honest feedback with regard to the operation, processes, procedures, employees, and equipment will be volunteered respectfully. This can be taken as unacceptable in an environment where honesty and principles are not cherished virtues. They can be perceived as intrusive and too firm by the direct management in their pursuit of excellence in both directions. The perseverance displayed by this type of leader can be perceived as harsh and not flexible, as this person, although capable, is not keen on playing office "games" or "politics" to achieve certain goals. They will not trade integrity for a position or a pat on the shoulder. They will not compromise on the expected excellence and will not allow anyone else to do so, which can create friction with other leaders with different mindsets, values, and approaches.

This type of leader will have everyone's best interest and well-being in focus, including the upper management, while performing duties and not shying away from self-sacrifice for the team. When wrong, they will admit their mistake, accept the repercussions, and work toward improvement in a timely manner.

9.2 "Wasn't me" type of leader

This type of leader will perform the job to the best of their abilities but with self-focus in mind. They will divert to self-preservation in case any difficulty is detected, which prevents them from exploring their maximum potential, as self-preservation consumes a lot of energy and attention. They will adhere to all company policies and keep their subordinates responsible for the same. They will communicate with the team and upper management but will not necessarily "stick the neck out" for anyone, even if the person is not at fault, due to fear of receiving repercussions themselves. This then prevents them from creating a stronger bond with the team and, subsequently, not receiving much respect from upper management. The team will notice their reservations and self-preservation and will not open up to the leader to the full extent possible to uphold trust and only offer limited respect. This leader will focus on the known and strive to stay in the comfort zone, not to risk exposure to the unknown. They consider taking new assignments and, especially, questioning the "status quo" as madness and unnecessary. As a result, they will not question anything from any form of authority, even if they disagree with it. This then could result in average, or even sometimes staggering, results within the team, as the drive to strive for excellence is shadowed by the fear of the unknown. They can maintain satisfactory levels of performance during a routine, but it will be challenging to produce the best results during high-stakes exceptional circumstances requiring on-the-go decision-making with limited information and resources. They will have the energy and will to comment on processes or company direction among their peers but will not support the same outside that circle. They will choose the safest approach in providing feedback on a subject they disagree with when asked by the authorities to give their opinions without upsetting anyone. This might result in not passing the right feedback and being lumped with unchanging circumstances as a result.

9.3 "I'm not here" type of leader

This type of leader is self-centered and plays the "game." They will not be interested in the well-being of anyone but themselves, although remaining aware of the need to maintain an illusion of caring. They will be involved in everything where they can present themselves as an achiever, but only if the tasks can be delegated and blame easily passed on to someone else in case of failure. They are not focused on the team or the company's goal; however, they will make an effort to find an area or activity in which they can thrive and show their "ingenuity." They will then explore that for self-promotion to achieve the goal of climbing up the company ladder. They will attend each and every function and gathering in the hope of being seen and exploring every opportunity to talk to upper management. They will make sure they are always involved in any discussion with upper management, offering safe comments for every topic. They will do a good job of dividing a team and picking individuals willing to take on extra workloads, increasing their own protection. This will then result in a broken team with divided groups within, with some individuals holding it all together with their exceptional performance, which will not be recognized. They will make sure they have a person reporting on all activities within the team and will rule by fear, not refraining from inflicting discipline, not shying away from proposing termination of employment to the relevant decision-makers, even for violations not warrant it.

This type of leader is a disease slowly eating away all the ingenuity, excellence, teamwork, and efficiency by destroying the team and lowering standards to those of division and incompetency.

ZORAN VIDOVIĆ

CHAPTER 10
Three basic attitudes

Like the leader types, the variety of attitudes displayed by employees cannot be fully encapsulated by this book, but we can capture an insight on the far sides of the spectrum, ranging from the best through the average to the worst. It serves as a guide, helping us detect modes of behavior gradually transitioning between the extremes on the said spectrum, thus providing us with necessary tools to help us react and address unprofessional behaviors and subsequently elevating the performance of individuals to expected levels. It can be an early sign of a company culture shift, which should not be ignored.

This projection applies to all employees; however, it complements the leader-type projection in our previous chapter, which together provides a greater variety of behaviors and characteristics as displayed by leaders across the board.

10.1 "Striving for excellence"

Employees displaying this type of attitude are focused on results and strive to deliver excellence. They can also display two opposing characteristics:

1. The "Take no prisoners" approach, which makes them focus on the final goal, while paying little or no attention to their coworkers or leaders. This is a brutal approach that delivers results but leaves little or no room

for cooperation and teamwork, which could result in a pyrrhic victory, depending on the job performed and required results.

2. The "Binom" (binomial) approach, where they focus on the best performance for the whole team, while not necessarily putting their interests first. This can be challenging and perhaps overwhelming for those members of the team not possessing the same stamina and determination, combined with the required character and skill set. This will be compensated for by team effort and shared workload.

Both approaches will deliver results, as individuals with this attitude are highly motivated and determined, with stamina and pursuit not deflating until the goal is reached.

However, sometimes, they are incapable of determining when to quit and shift focus, as they are hard to frighten, discourage, or overwhelm, even with the most challenging tasks. They can get frustrated with the company, leadership, and coworkers if they are not understood and supported in their quest. They are usually quick in problem resolution as they are always thinking ahead and in multiple directions, combining the possibilities of different outcomes to any specific scenario. They thrive in fast-paced, high-stakes situations where they need to engage their full capacity and come up with problem resolutions.

Individuals with this attitude have all the qualities required for advancing up the ladder but are not likely to be presented with the opportunity due to not being understood by the higher authority, combined with their fear of being outperformed.

We need to recognize this attitude and steer it in the right direction to complement and boost team performance in support of the company's mission.

10.2 "Looking for a purpose"

Employees displaying this type of attitude are actively involved in company activities and strive to be part of the "family." They strive to perform up to the required standard and are willing to participate in all activities offered by the company. They are enthusiastic and energetic and seem to be constantly happy and satisfied, although they do not necessarily exceed expectations. They can relate to the company mission and are easily influenced and molded by the company, to such an extent that they suspend or even abandon personal beliefs to fit into the company's social construct. This can be both good and bad, depending on the circumstances, as they are not eager to challenge the direction imposed by the company or the leadership, regardless of the outcome, due to their submissive nature. They are somewhat interested in advancement within the company, although it is not their main drive. Their main drive is belonging and having a purpose in a society they are comfortable with.

These individuals can form bonds and settle within a team of like-minded individuals; however, they will be reluctant to voice any opinion that might jeopardize their status. It is belonging that they are striving for and are happy and proud to display in public, defending the company from all criticism. They are good, loyal employees, willing to execute tasks with little or no question, regardless of the potential impact, as they do not challenge authority. They might be susceptible to manipulation by their managers when challenged on their loyalty and performance due to fear of jeopardizing their employment and their need to belong to the "family."

We need to address this attitude by empowering positive change and self-development to achieve improved performance, advancing communication, expressing opinions, and delivering better results.

10.3 "Just in it for a ride"

Employees displaying this type of attitude are not looking for a purpose or belonging, which could be due to several reasons, including:

1. They could be overqualified for the job and consider it to be a temporary assignment.

2. They could be underqualified and not able to understand the job and settle in.

3. They have retired from a previous career and consider this job to be additional income, without attachments and too much involvement.

4. They are disgruntled employees who do not trust the management and do not believe in the company's mission.

Whichever way, they are not willing or able to perform at the required level or add to team performance as they do not feel sufficient enthusiasm and trust in the company. It is especially important to recognize and address such a situation to prevent it from affecting the rest of the employees and, subsequently, the company.

We need to address it in a way that allows the employee to express their feedback and reasoning behind the underperformance. We need to understand whether the employee has understood the job's role. Perhaps a conversation and setting expectations can bring the employee back on track and see them actively involved in the process. We can then equip the employee with the required skills and set a focus on the important aspects that need improvement while expanding their existing satisfactory performance. We should be direct and honest while communicating clear expectations along with emphasizing our support. We are the critical part of this process, which, if done correctly, will result in one of three outcomes:

1. The employee will understand the expectations and importance of performing as per the company standard, while completing all required tasks. The employee will then feel accepted and appreciated, with boosted enthusiasm, thereby elevating their performance and settling them back within the team.

2. The employee will understand the company's expectations and the required skills that need to be obtained, which we hope will result in honest self-reflection and the realization that they are not ready for their current role. They might decide they need a change and vacate the position, which might be the best outcome for all, considering the circumstances.

3. The employee might reason with us and decide to reveal the cause of disassociation from the company's mission. This way we can get honest feedback and the opportunity to rectify the situation, by addressing their stated concerns. We might even reveal opportunities for improvement in a different segment of the company, whether management support, procedures, equipment auditing performance and performance review, or even hiring process.

However, it turns out that this attitude will need to be attended to and elevated if the employee is to contribute to our ultimate goals. If we fail to recognize the problem, we are running a risk of team failure in delivering our required results supporting the company's mission.

ZORAN VIDOVIĆ

CHAPTER 11
Combination of basic leader types and attitudes

As we have already mentioned in the previous chapters, we can recognize three basic types of leaders, along with three basic attitudes of employees, which, combined, give us a more in-depth overview of the potential performance spectrum. Now, these types, as described, are basic and can have a variety of subtypes on the spectrum in each category. These types can also be combined, forming a variety of complex individuals on a wide spectrum of characters and performance levels. We will now expand on this and show the interaction between the characteristics of various leader types along with different attitudes.

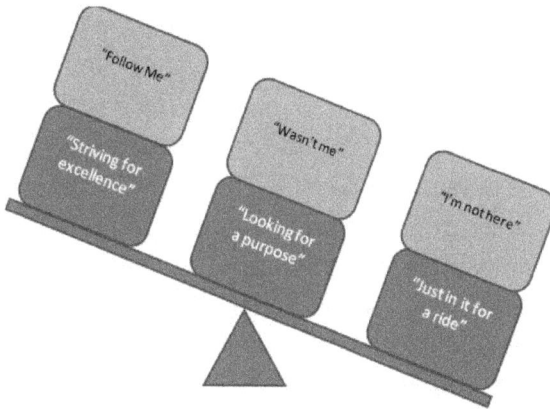

Figure 11.1. *Relationship between leader type and attitude, showing how the negative combination outweighs the positive and impacts company culture.*

11.1 "Follow me" leader with "Striving for excellence" attitude

This combination will create an individual who will shoot for the stars and take the company in the direction of success. We are looking for this kind of drive to boost us toward our set goals. This combination of character and attitude will provide enough energy and ingenuity to pull along the others while resolving every obstacle on the way to the top. This is a person who thrives in difficult situations that require focus, energy, and leadership that bring out the best from everyone in the team. This person takes ownership of the situation and works toward the company mission while keeping in focus the well-being of subordinates and colleagues.

11.2 "Wasn't me" leader with "Looking for purpose" attitude

This type of leader will assist in getting the company in the right direction but will remain completely dependent on the leading force. This leader is not a driving force but can relate to the mission and thrive under the umbrella of a superior leader. This person can assist in "holding the fort" and making decisions in controlled, familiar segments of the operation while waiting for confirmation and approval from upper management, particularly for any risky decision pertaining to a new set of circumstances. This is especially applicable during challenging, new, and unfamiliar operations requiring initiative, innovation, and ingenuity accompanied by greater risk associated with new processes or directions, such as the expansion or growth of the company.

11.3 "I'm not here" leader with "Just in it for a ride" attitude

This combination is like an anchor that will drag everyone down and slow the process of achieving the set goal. This type of person offers a problem for every solution and keeps constantly pushing a personal cloud of negativity and skepticism toward any and every possible outcome. This is not an achiever nor a motivator focused on the mission. It is a person who will scatter the energy and focus of the team, preventing it from achieving the set goal, even if the resolution is within reach. It might make you wonder if such leaders are doing it on purpose or if it is simply an inability to perform. It could be a combination of both; however, they will remain present in order to accept appreciation and rewards for any results achieved by the team.

Those three combinations of leadership type and attitude are three extremes that represent the best, average, and worst we may encounter. We can find a variety of leaders who might be leaning toward each side of the spectrum. The danger is if we do not identify those signs that lean toward the worst side of the spectrum, we might find our productivity and results diminishing.

We could have a leader with a positive leader type adopting a negative attitude, which might result in a change of leadership style for the worse.

We need to look into the reasons for inadequate performance and identify appropriate approaches to elevate it. This might be due to insecurity, a toxic working environment, or perhaps former bad experiences inhibiting them from expressing themselves.

Whatever the cause, we need to establish a culture where this sort of reluctance will be noticed and attended to in an attempt to get everyone on the preferred optimal level of performance for their personal and professional growth and, subsequently, in order to achieve the company's mission.

	"Follow me – Striving for excellence"	"Wasn't me – Looking for purpose"	"I'm not here – Just in it for a ride"
Strengths	Highly motivated, focused, and inspirational Takes ownership, supports, and motivates others Thrives in challenges and focuses on collective success	Reliable and stable in familiar conditions Loyal and supportive under strong leadership Helps maintain operational consistency	May perform basic tasks if closely supervised Occasionally helps maintain routine operations
Weaknesses	Risk of burnout from overcommitment, especially when not supported Can be impatient with slower team members May dominate discussions or initiatives, and challenge authority due to strong will and clear vision	Lacks initiative and self-direction Hesitant in new or high-risk situations Dependent on others for motivation and purpose	Lacks drive, vision, and accountability Negative and resistant to change Avoids responsibility and blames others
Opportunities	Can mentor others and build a leadership culture Drives innovation, growth, and change Strengthens company culture and morale	Can grow with a clear purpose and mentoring Useful in stable or structured environments Potential to develop moderate leadership skills	May show limited improvement through coaching, supervision and reassignment Could contribute in a non-leadership or support role, under supervision
Threats	May be perceived as assertive or dominant when not supported Risk of team overreliance on one strong leader May lose interest if not challenged by the position	Risk of stagnation and disengagement May slow decision-making in fast-paced settings Could fail to create and inspire a team Susceptible to manipulation by leadership	Creates a toxic culture and high turnover Reduces productivity and damages morale Threatens long-term organizational success
Conclusion	**Optimal blend of drive and attitude, fueling progress and inspiring others**	**Dependable but lacks initiative and requires guidance to reach full potential**	**Liability to morale and performance, necessitating decisive intervention or reassignment**

Figure 11.2. *SWOT analysis of the combinations of basic leader types and attitudes.*

11.4   The effect a position of power has on different types of leaders and employees

We can observe the shift between behaviors, before and after stepping into the leadership role, for most employees. Some shifts are positive, and some are negative, with both having a great impact on the employees and the company. We can detect three major shifts:

1. **Positive**, in the sense that the employee has obtained detailed knowledge of the new leadership role with a deep understanding of the responsibilities and expectations. These employees have formed a healthy opinion of their role and decided on a laudable approach, which is being open to suggestions from every direction. These employees are conscious of their limitations but also of the opportunities for growth and development, having a clear understanding that such growth can be achieved and boosted with help from their subordinates. They are aware of their flaws and shortcomings and are ready to listen and consider input from all employees with the best intention for their development and growth. They are willing to admit their mistakes and learn from their shortcomings while expanding their knowledge and developing themselves along with their teams, subsequently excelling in supporting the company's mission.

2. **Neutral.** This employee does have an overall understanding of the responsibilities and expectations while also having a harder time accepting them. This might be due to a premature promotion or an assignment to a temporary position. They are pleased with the position and all the perks coming with it; however,

they are not fully ready and consequently might have a limited ability to develop additional skills that could help them achieve all required goals. The position might potentially result in a "freeze" reaction, which limits their performance and learning capacity due to an overwhelmed reaction to new responsibilities, all depending on the workload and the level of cooperation and guidance from their fellow colleagues, along with support from the upper management. This effect does not render a person unsusceptible to the positive support from fellow colleagues and subordinates, which helps to alleviate negative aspects and provides a platform for success.

3. **Negative.** This effect makes the employees more convinced of their superiority over others, as they start their leader's journey with a twisted self-image of a capable, complete, developed, and undisputed leader. They are not receptive to advice volunteered by fellow colleagues or subordinates or from upper management, as their self-image prevents them from admitting mistakes. They are unlikely to accept criticism and most likely will despise the person giving it, as they are convinced that their way is the only way. Once they are cornered by their flawed decision-making process, they will create a different reality where their twisted logic identifies the suspect in the form of someone else while giving themselves an alibi for their actions. They will project their shortcomings and flaws onto someone else and convince themselves of that reality, which makes them extremely convincing to others. They will maintain a calm posture even when confronted with the evidence disputing their claim, as they are convinced of their innocence. They are just not capable of conceiving the

possibility that they are currently not at the desired, self-projected level, which then leads to repetitive behavior resulting in negative impacts on their subordinates, fellow colleagues, upper management, and the company.

All of these behaviors, mostly triggered by their position of power fueled by their character specifics, can be interconnected and shift from one end of the spectrum to the other.

The shift can also happen because of pressure or stress, an accident, or a highly disturbing catastrophe, which is overwhelming for the said individuals.

We have all worked with a colleague or have managed individuals who have changed their behavior drastically after promotion. They made such an extensive shift from their previous behavior that they became almost unrecognizable. They shifted from always challenging and complaining about certain tasks, procedures, and authority into the undisputed authority enforcing exactly the same tasks and procedures without allowing for any questioning of the same. They turned into an unapproachable leader with little or no appreciation for the well-being of their subordinates. They became the leader they never liked. This phenomenon is perplexing, awkward, and interesting at the same time. It just shows us the complexity of human beings, along with the importance and influence of human behavior on the company's mission.

11.5 Employee motivation dependence:

11.5.1 Background

- **Personal background** consists of our experienced life situations which build character and establish our persona from an early age, starting from our family relations. We carry that with us, as it has shaped us. It includes positive and negative experiences that both mold our reality and set expectations, with a profound sense of self-preservation, or a lack of it. It strongly influences our basic needs. It will move us from being open or closed to new situations and emotionally equipped—or not—to weather storms in our pursuit of happiness in a desired form.

- **Educational background** is set of learned skills, behaviors and experiences embedded in us during education. It is deeply interconnected with our personal background as the interaction with our peers and teachers leaves profound marks on us. It can complement the personal background or negatively influence it, creating friction and collision between the two. It then could result in a constant struggle between the two sets of us; our raised selves and our educated selves.

- **Professional background** usually comes in addition to the above, but it could be interconnected depending on the time we became immersed in working relationships. We can add additional friction to the two above by building professional experience contradicting the two. This is then an even more complicated situation as it will take great time and effort to reflect and find the true inner self, which will complement the current image or shatter it.

11.5.2 Expectations

- **Personal expectations** are somewhat hard to measure and could be more emotional than embedded in reality. Personal disappointments in achieving those can affect our ability to pursue professional goals as they have exhausted our energy and blurred our focus.

- **Professional expectations** are usually more measurable but could be also highly connected with our emotions. Getting a raise is a measurable experience, while getting a promotion is both measurable and emotional, and getting an unexpected appraisal from colleagues and leaders is more of an emotional experience. Either way, all of the above should positively influence us and set us on the path to success and growth, while negative experiences will do the opposite.

11.5.3 Self-esteem

Self-esteem is highly dependent on the above-mentioned backgrounds and expectations as it can result in a fluctuation of our self-esteem depending on the newly presented personal and professional challenges. We might see that in individuals perceived as firm and brave achievers in professional life who have a completely different approach to their personal life and vice versa. So, self-esteem is dependent on multiple elements and can fluctuate with our growth.

We need to understand the complexity of employee motivation and equip ourselves with patience and perseverance to be able to guide and motivate every member of our team in a positive direction by addressing those elements holding them back. And yes, it does require us to utilize psychology during the process, as every human being is different, with different backgrounds, experiences, expectations, and self-esteem. This is why every leader should invest in developing the ability to recognize and address the limitations or faults of all employees while repressing any potential feelings of resentment, disrespect, or disgust that could arise. We need to strive for excellence, ingenuity, and perseverance by beginning with ourselves and understanding the complexity of human beings with all the influences presented by various elements. Once we elevate ourselves above the holding grip of disappointments and paralyzing fear, we can help others do the same.

11.6 The effect the working environment has on leaders and employees

The working environment has a significant impact on each employee and, in the long run, even each leader's type, by changing a person's character and personality as a result of immense and prolonged influences, such as stress. It is a continual influence that might make us fluctuate by switching between the positive and negative sides of the spectrum. It all depends on the prevailing leadership styles in the company, combined, when negative, with the lack of supporting culture and no mechanism for monitoring and detecting undesired behaviors and leadership styles. We can have instances where a change of CEO brings a change in company culture, gradually influencing the mission, resulting in a concentration of, and preference for, the new leadership style to the point of eradicating the old, previously preferred style. A new "sheriff" in town, implementing new rules, can turn the company away from the mission. This then creates fertile ground for confusion and feelings of hopelessness as the known is now undesired, and the unknown becomes desired. Everyone will react differently to this situation depending on their leader's type, motivation, and attitude. Obviously, the environment has suddenly become unknown and potentially hostile, which brings another unknown to the equation in the form of perspective, depending on the new expectations for each position, known as the Position Effect. All of this can then influence motivation and result in changes in attitude depending on the level of acceptance of the proposed changes.

An example would be a stressful environment such as military operations where individuals, especially those in power, once placed under immense stress and under an expectation of desired results, can make decisions influencing human lives and even eradicating them, which they might later on regret and find absolutely unacceptable and out of character, although the same might be accepted, desired, and glorified within their cohort. This trip into an unknown and probably undesired leadership style results in personal conflicts, which can have deep impacts on individuals.

We should also never underestimate the power of peer pressure as it could also greatly affect and drive decisions away from the personal norm.

We have examples throughout history, especially in the 20th century leading up to today, where a change in behavior happened to whole nations, with some groups within identifying and adopting the most horrific and undesired norms and behaviors, formerly unacceptable and inconceivable by anyone, both within and outside those cultures.

So, the power of the environment is immense and needs to be understood and appreciated as it has continued, and will continue, to influence companies and societies as a whole. No one is immune to this as every person finds themselves insidiously subject to social pressures and the normalization of aberrant behavior through observing and gradually becoming part of widespread and new policies, expectations, and demands;

this effect negative and devastating change for that individual, company, and society as a whole.

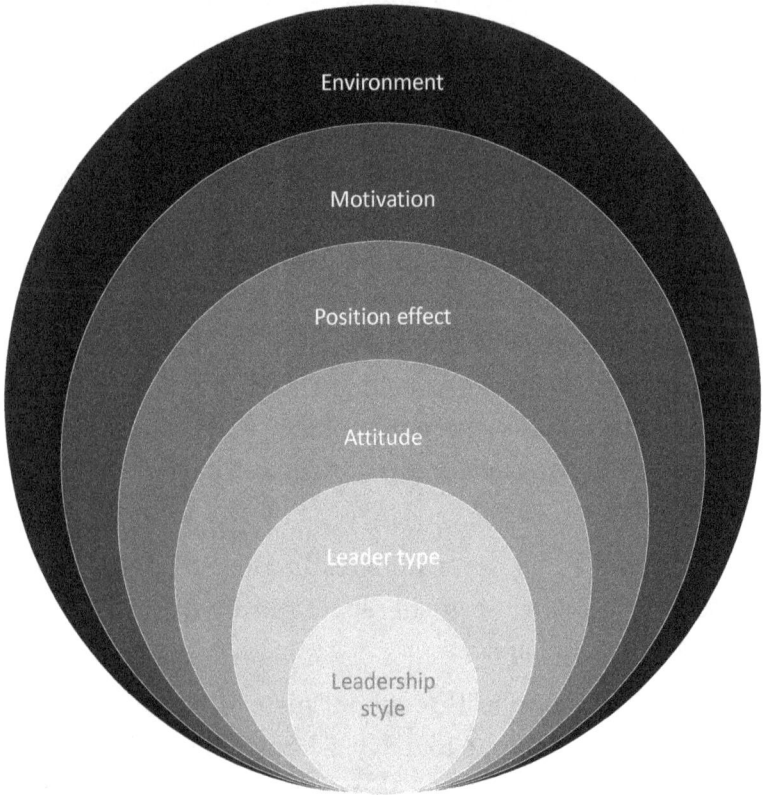

Figure 11.3. *Layers of influence on leadership style*

This chart shows the complexity of a leader's position, which is influenced by a person's character, attitude, and motivation, along with the reality of power and responsibility introduced by the position and complemented by the environment. This needs to be understood to begin to peel off the layers, to reveal all the complexity of a person and their reaction to outside elements while being shaped within them.

We can have a "Follow me" leader with a "Striving for

excellence" attitude under an immense hostile working environment, potentially turning into an "I'm not here" leader with a "Just in it for a ride" attitude. So, the environment can negatively influence leadership style regardless of the desired leader type and attitude.

Understanding this provides us an opportunity to positively influence people on the individual level and help them grow. It is surprising how much we can achieve by adopting the right approach to presenting employees with opportunities for growth and improvement. We can have the worst-performing employee turned into our leading force, bursting with dedication and enthusiasm. Leaders are no exception, as they face pressure from all sides, which may cause them to switch between different leadership styles, affecting their motivation and attitude toward the position, company, and employees. Good leaders don't just lead; they develop others into leaders.

It is like flying a kite with five strings attached, controlled by five people speaking different languages. If we do not find a common language or a translator, it will be hard to synchronize everyone, pulling the strings in the right direction, and the kite will crash. Looking from afar, it will be clear what the cause was, but for each person involved, it will be another person's fault, as everyone will be convinced that they performed to the best of their ability. So, individually, they will all feel right, as they gave their best, just not in line with others and not in the required direction to capture the true wind. The leader is the translator and responsible for synchronizing the performances of all five individuals (various influences) by making sure they all individually understand in which direction to fly a kite (the company's mission) and how each individual performance influences others (direction and preferred method of execution).

So, as leaders, we need to self-reflect and detect which

influences are negatively affecting us and dragging us away from the desired performance. We can do this by rising above our influences and looking at ourselves from a distance, which will help us detect which influence is preventing our "kite" from flying. Is it our motivation, position effect, leadership type, environment, or our attitude? We can then change it to adjust to the required standard and the desired leadership style, complementing the company's mission.

This is not an easy process, as each of us is the hardest person to change. So, often, we resist change, regardless of how convinced we are of its necessity.

We need to understand that everyone else probably has the same resistance to change and might not respond positively to it, so we need to tailor our approach for each individual to communicate in an understandable and acceptable way, which will help that person understand the benefits of a change and not feel that they are being unfairly coerced. This way, we have a greater, more positive, and longer-lasting effect on individuals and their performance.

Understanding others starts with understanding ourselves. We need to detect what triggers us and what makes us cooperate. We then need to understand that every person is an individual, and a specific approach will need to be taken to reach them. "One size fits all" will not work on everyone, and it is mostly short-lived, even on those it does work on. It can be perceived as coercive as it does not recognize the needs of individuals.

This is especially important to understand in the new millennium, as the new working cohort is more sensitive than the one from the last millennium. What was once accepted and understood as a norm is now absolute taboo, from smoking in the office to making inappropriate jokes and behaviors bordering on bullying. People are more self-conscious and demand to be treated with respect and dignity, which has triggered a change in desired leadership styles from "do as I say" to "follow me." Although this is a positive change, it brings different challenges, as people might become overly sensitive and self-focused, which makes the leadership role ever more demanding, requiring a variety of social and communication skills to be able to reach every individual. It can be tiring, and we need to understand when we have exhausted all opportunities to positively influence an employee's behavior and performance as, after all, we are not their private counselors and life coaches but their leaders who will need to bring measurable results within set time frames.

So, we need to exhaust all opportunities for developing improvement, but we need to communicate the expectations and repercussions if the employees do not respond to positive input and guidance. We are all adults and have agreed to certain terms of employment for monetary gain, which needs to be adhered to, but with the utmost respect and appreciation for the employees, but also leaders, and the company. Not everyone possesses the same abilities, so we need to be aware of that too. Sometimes, we just have individuals who are not able to perform at the required standard, and we need to determine why to be able to address the matter.

Here's a hint at the behavioral signs suggesting a possible approach in detecting reasons for an unsynchronized performance:

1. **Not capable of performing day-to-day tasks, but excels in challenging tasks.**

   We need to determine the possible cause triggering such behavior and invest time and effort to assist in rectifying it:

a) Boredom? Why? Is the person about to retire? Is the job presenting challenges far below the person's capabilities? If so, we need to determine those capabilities by exploring with them what might be more challenging and demanding tasks, or possible positions.

b) No incentive for repetitive and unchallenging tasks? Why? Does the person consider their current job a temporary job due to superior performance abilities? Has the person been overlooked during succession planning? Was the person moved down from a higher position? All of the above need to be answered and appropriate steps taken to bring the performance up to the desired level.

c) Wrong leadership approach? Personality clash? Is the person not recognized for the work they do, nor acknowledged for positive input? We need to determine the exact trigger and rectify it.

d) Negative team influence? Not supporting the team? Has the person assimilated into the team? Any clashes with particular team members? This is important to be recognized and rectified immediately, since it can negatively influence other team members.

2. **Sudden drastic change in behavior and performance:**

a) This could be caused by a promotion as the feeling of power might have negatively affected their reasoning and their personality. They could be in a situation where they realize they are not equipped to implement desired changes, as the same were generated based on a mistaken perception of reality, coupled with a romantic view of their new position, power, and responsibilities. This could then encourage them to adopt well known, but previously resented behavior traits and an unfavorable leadership style, purely because it is familiar and comfortable. Addressing this is imperative as this behavior can negatively affect the team, especially if it is the same team the said leader was part of before promotion.

b) Could it be caused by personal circumstances beyond our influence? We need to make an effort to talk to the employee and show empathy. Sometimes an honest conversation can remove the feeling of hopelessness and loneliness, which might help people to pull together and bring them back on track.

c) Caused by a recent change within the organization? New responsibilities? Pay cut? New leader? We need to determine the cause and work toward the resolution, which very well might be out of our reach, but the effort will count. We might be able to elevate the concern to the responsible department and help the employee argue their case.

d) Caused by tectonic shifts in the market, due to global dynamics, such as a pandemic? We might not be able to assist much, but we can show interest and understanding by acknowledging the situation and the negative impact on the employee. We can reassure the employee that we will communicate any new information and have the employee's interests in mind during decision-making.

3. **Underperforming and not responding to feedback:**
   a) Which segments of someone's performance are not at

the required level? Did the feedback capture the reason for poor performance? Has it been clearly communicated, along with clear support, expectations and possible repercussions? If so, we need to speak with the employee and understand the reason behind the continued underperformance, establishing a clear understanding that persisting with a poor performance will result in professional/career repercussions, once we have exhausted all other options, namely advice, guidance, retraining, etc.

b) Has the person expressed potential reasons for the underperformance? Can we assist in elevating their performance? Are they willing and able to accept the same and elevate their performance?

11.7 What to remember

It is important for all of us to understand and be on the lookout for our own fatigue and drop in readiness and energy to maintain our performance at the highest standard, supporting our approach and leadership style. We need to detect when we are on the verge of a performance drop with narrowed vision and impaired reasoning capabilities. We should not react precipitously when deciding on an employee's performance feedback and, subsequently, their future. We need to be in control of our emotions if we are to conduct conscientious and fact-driven analysis with conclusions embedded in reality, in line with our set company mission and standard. We must then display a consistent standard in our own performance and decision-making, which will be respected by our colleagues and employees, even when they do not fully agree with our decision. It gives everyone confidence in our integrity, empowering them to accept our authority. Leaders need to understand that true authority and leadership cannot just come from a position but, more importantly, from a style, poise, intelligence, empathy, selflessness, and courage that colleagues and subordinates respect, understanding that we hold ourselves accountable to the same standards that we demand from them. This is pure gold and indestructible as it cannot be taken away from us as long as we have a disciplined continuum in maintaining this standard. It will not necessarily make people like us, but it will help them respect us. Remember, we will also be leading and working alongside individuals who are less focused on excellence and integrity but rather on their own personal success and image.

11.8 So, how do we manage teams?

Do we expect exactly the same from each employee, or should we reevaluate our expectations? Obviously, we need to tailor our approach and develop our leadership style, which helps identify the strengths and weaknesses of each employee. We also need to be careful not to overly focus on weaknesses and end up dulling strengths while not elevating the weaknesses to a desired level. We need to find balance. That is the key.

So, how do we decide what to focus on? We look at the team and decide on the required tasks to be performed as a team, and then we look at the individual task performances of each team member to identify their strengths and weaknesses. Remember, we are managing a team and not a group of cloned individuals or robots, so it is expected that we will encounter a spectrum of performances across the board.

We then analyze the relationship between an individual's strengths and weaknesses and the influence they have on team tasks and the company's mission. The question we should ask ourselves is, do we really need this individual to strengthen their weakness? Is their strength perhaps casting a shadow on the weakness, a shadow perhaps on other people's strengths too? If so, is it a wise business decision to elevate the weaknesses on behalf of the strength? Perhaps it sounds ludicrous, but our job is to lead a team toward the set company's mission and not to make a uniform group of individuals. Obviously, in some operations, this might be needed due to the specifics of the job; for example, the conformity of appearance and behavior in the military, police services, marine, and aviation sectors, or private protection services, where uniformity is strived for to showcase professionalism and cohesion. We should not confuse those requirements with all aspects of those jobs, as we need to bring results, and appearance is just a segment of it. We need to strive for content and not only window-dressing.

If you have ever belonged to the above-mentioned industries, you have probably met individuals with appearances complementing the projected image of a perfect employee, but unfortunately, their performance was anything but perfect. So, we need to bridge this gap and make sure we have all individuals' strengths further widened and explored to compensate for any weaknesses. For example, if we are managing a team of individuals performing duties in a marine or military setting and we discover individuals with elevated technical/tactical abilities but limited communication/social abilities or vice versa. What are we going to do? Have them work on their weaknesses or further widen their abilities? This will depend on the individual strengths and weaknesses of each team member. Obviously, if all our individuals have superior technical abilities but weak social abilities, then we will need to engage in changing the ratio. If, on the other hand, we have a mix of individuals, some with elevated technical abilities and some with elevated social abilities, then we can organize our team members to complement each other and get the best from them while empowering them to improve upon their shortcomings.

A few quotes from General Patton sum it up quite nicely:

"If everyone is thinking alike, then somebody isn't thinking."

"Do not try to make circumstances fit your plans. Make plans that fit the circumstances."

We are responsible for the team and need to build a team of individuals by exploring their strengths, weaknesses, and limits, not by necessarily getting everyone on the same level in every segment. Why is this approach important? Because we ensure frustration, boredom, and lack of interest do not afflict our highly capable individuals, who are often characterized as misfits due to their inability to accept what they perceive as trivial. So, why risk it? In fact, let's benefit from it and use it. Identify those individuals and have them work for you. Have them excel in what they do and gradually bring them into the other segments of the operation. On the other hand, we will have individuals at the lower end of the spectrum of competence who need repetitive guidance and direction if they are to adapt to the norm. We will gradually get these individuals to the required level as valuable team members who are aware of their limitations and the necessary remedial action. The wisdom is in not overdoing this, meaning we need to be cautious not to tolerate employees within the lower end of the spectrum of competency to exist dependent on the performance of the highly capable employees who then might develop a feeling of being exploited by the company if they are continuously expected to perform the most demanding tasks and even to rectify other employees' mistakes. So, yes, we will have both and everything in between, and we will need to make them work together and complement each other's performances. That is what we do as leaders.

Above all, we need to understand that we need to change and adapt our leadership style depending on circumstances and presented challenges. We are constantly evolving and changing, so we need to monitor that change to prevent it from taking us in the wrong direction. It can happen quickly and unnoticeably, and before we have time to realize we have changed as a person, with different behaviors and leadership styles, ones that we might not be proud of.

Obviously, there are expectations and standards that must be established and followed in order for businesses to be productive and successful. We need to strive for the best and provide support for everyone to be able to achieve our goals. Then, it is on the individuals to take responsibility for not achieving our mission and accept the consequences of their actions. We need to understand and accept differences, empower people to cherish those, and encourage them to adopt all the positive aspects while exposing their strengths to others. However, we need to respect the freedom of every human being to not participate in the process or to make insufficient effort to achieve set goals. It is their right, and it needs to be respected within the widest context but dealt with locally because it is not their right to feel this way and continue to occupy a team position.

We also need to be conscious of those unable to perform at the required level due to their limited abilities. We need to set in place mechanisms and support to allow everyone to grow, but we should not strive to pull and push those individuals whose reality is the opposite of the rest of the world. We need to be honest and realistic about everyone's performance and have the wisdom to understand when it's time for people to move on and explore other opportunities.

No point in beating a dead horse.

CHAPTER 12

The correlation between company culture and prevailing leadership styles

I f the negative style of leadership is allowed to prevail, we will risk creating multiple cultures within the company, which will then create hostile working environments and destroy motivation.

12.1 Leader cult

This prevents any subordinates from expressing their concern or even coming to the realization that there is one who doesn't accord with the leader's performance and decisions. This is due to the culture of undisputed leaders who are always right as the company promotes them to a level of unquestionable authority, preventing any challenge by the subordinates due to the fear of being wrong, ridicule by colleagues and leaders, and facing down unchecked and unsupervised power.

There are some industries where a certain position holds a lot of power and influence over the operation and employees' lives, which cannot be taken away due to the nature of the position and environment, one such being a maritime or aviation captain. However, there needs to be a counterweight that balances power and limits the possibility of abuse of power. And this needs to be driven by the company using various tools such as bridge resource management. We need to understand that such positions require a firm decision-maker who could present a scary obstacle for any other officer, especially junior officers, in expressing their concern with certain decisions, even when lives are in danger.

We can also come across senior officers, reserved in their approach to voicing their opinion, which might contradict captains, as they will fear jeopardizing their chances for promotion. This is natural and happens frequently, which is why communication and teamwork are the key elements of success that need to be established by the company with a clear policy governing it.

We have examples of marine and aviation casualties, with numerous lives lost, due to a captain's poor decision-making, unquestioned or challenged by any other officer onboard, even when the catastrophe was imminent and unavoidable. One example is the Costa Concordia casualty, resulting in the death of 32 persons and 157 injured. As concluded by the Italian Ministry of Infrastructures and Transport, human factors characterized this marine casualty.[26]

It is hard to be the person who points at the elephant in the room when everyone else seems not able to see it or does not want to, but we need to create an environment that supports opposing opinions instead of sanctioning them in order to prevent catastrophic events. This does not only apply to maritime and aviation industries but everywhere.

---

26. https://www.mitma.gob.es/recursos_mfom/2012costaconcordia.pdf

12.2 The end justifies the means

A company culture where financial gain is the only measure of success, and the path to achieving it is left for everyone to decide on then creates a "free for all" culture where anything goes, as long as the final goal is achieved. The "don't ask, don't tell" mentality can produce results, but at what price for everyone involved: society and the environment?

One example is the fall of ENRON in 2001, which was, at the time, the biggest corporate bankruptcy in the U.S. with 63.4 billion in assets.[27] It was revealed that the company switched to MTM (mark to market) accounting, which helped them hide losses and boost the appearance of profitability, which was signed off on by their accounting firms. This just shows the level of greed across the board, along with the blind obedience and persistence in the modus operandi perpetrated by all involved.

12.3 Quid pro quo

You will get somewhere only if you scratch the right back. This type of culture prevents people from expressing themselves and achieving their full potential. Anyone excelling will be considered a threat to the set standard and is unlikely to be accepted by their colleagues or leaders. They will not be granted the opportunity to advance since they shed light on the poor performance of others. Leaders enjoy the benefits of such a culture and control the behavior of subordinates, making sure no one gets out of line and steps on anyone's toes in their

---

27. https://www.investopedia.com/terms/e/enron.asp

pursuit of real results and transparency. This environment could foster other unwanted behaviors, such as various types of harassment, including sexual harassment and bullying. An example is a quid pro quo ruling in 1976 at the end of the case of Williams v. Saxbe.[28] [29]

All of the above is influenced by the herd mentality, which is susceptible to the behavior of a "strong alpha" subject or a behavior of majority-peer pressure. This is why we need to monitor the culture and tendency for some leaders to move across the spectrum toward an undesirable leadership style and make sure we empower all employees to speak up.

We have the ultimate responsibility of creating a culture and environment in which we cherish the diversity of humankind and include people with different values and beliefs. We need to empower everyone to fulfill their duties to achieve the highest performance standard while cherishing their character. We must also understand the limitations of individuals and teams in meeting the established standard using the available processes and tools, while allowing and respecting refusal to participate. We need to understand and accept the employee's personal decision in not performing, evolving, growing, and developing while respecting their integrity by holding them accountable to the set standard across the board.

None of this is an easy answer. Ultimately, we have to establish rules and policies that give the company and its employees the greatest chance of success while making allowance for those occasions when bad apples disrupt performance. There is no avoiding moral courage. It will so often require the

---

28. https://en.wikipedia.org/wiki/
Sexual_harassment_in_the_workplace_in_the_United_States

29. https://www.eeoc.gov/data/
sexual-harassment-our-nations-workplaces

courage of the moral individual to take a risk and step out of line to highlight injustice. That brings personal danger, hence the term "moral courage."

ZORAN VIDOVIĆ

CHAPTER 13
Conclusion

13.1 The company's responsibility

It is the company's responsibility to create its culture and climate by utilizing certain elements, some of which are highlighted in this book, to select, hire, train, promote, and supervise the right individuals for the right positions based on each individual's ability to perform each job, to defined levels, under clear and transparent conditions. This is achieved by setting unambiguous expectations for each position, along with the required qualifications, supported by complementing procedures, processes, systems, and equipment. We need to monitor the performance of each individual at all levels, giving concise feedback in order to boost performance and elevate employees' self-esteem, motivation, attitude, proficiency, and qualifications, as required to advance through the company, while opening each employee's perception of their opportunities for growth and self-development. It will be important to create a culture that cherishes creativity, ingenuity, excellence, perseverance, and dedication to achieving set goals while maintaining the highest standards of environmental and social health. We should not strive for profit only, as doing so turns everything and everyone into a commodity, removing humanity from the picture. We need to understand that an economy fueled by business needs to serve the higher purpose of bringing people together for the exchange of experiences and ideas, thereby supporting the development of human relations and societies for the benefit of the human race, with cautious, caring, and respectful relationships within our environment.

Every enterprise needs to serve the greater good and have a mission other than generating profit. This can only be achieved if everyone involved is on the same page. To achieve this, we need to create a society that respects differences and works toward the common goal with respect to every person in the process. We need to establish communication channels that are protected from distortion and not tainted by personal interests, as the greater good should come above personal interests and especially above profit.

To be able to achieve this, we need to establish the company's mission, vision, and company culture with core values in line with the God-given rights and responsibilities of each human being and look at nature as a gift and not our asset.

Only then will profit come as a result of competency, excellence, ingenuity, and innovation as it serves the greater good.

13.2 The leader's responsibility

A leader is an employee with additional responsibilities and tasks to deliver results in line with the company's mission, vision, and standard. By accepting this position, every leader is accepting all the perks and responsibilities that come with it. The responsibility, unlike the different tasks and assignments, cannot be delegated and stays with the leader regardless of potential inability or reluctance to accept it. Once the position is accepted, the responsibility is accepted as well.

That being said, the leader is morally and ethically

responsible for monitoring and responding to any deviations from the norm, regardless of whether they relate to a company's mission, vision, standard, or laws and regulations.

Communication is of the essence and needs to be cherished to maintain an open flow of information and ideas to take the company and its employees on the path to success.

Every leader has the responsibility to develop teams in line with the company's mission and vision, providing the same benefits to society. Leaders are expected to have great moral values and not to shy away from executing decisions that could expose them to the scrutiny of not like-minded and motivated individuals, including upper management. Leaders should notice and acknowledge each member of their team, with their strengths and weaknesses, aligning them with the path of success and empowering them to develop and succeed. Leaders should voice their opinions and speak up if they notice any sign of power abuse or deviation from positive and acceptable behaviors on every level within the company. They should maintain the highest level of integrity and moral and ethical principles, which need to be reflected in their decision-making process.

Remember, a true leader is constantly balancing between being fired and being promoted.

If you are playing it safe, you are not a leader!

13.3 The employee's responsibility

Each employee needs to speak up about any hint of power abuse and misalignment with the company's mission and vision. Employees need to understand their rights and responsibilities along with the rights and responsibilities of their leaders to prevent power abuse and destruction of the positive company culture. Employees are also responsible for delivering their best performance according to their abilities in line with the company's mission, vision, and standards. They have agreed to certain terms and conditions of employment, with perks and responsibilities that need to be respected and adhered to.

Self-reflection questions for Leaders

1. Why am I doing this job?

   a) Money

      ☐ As a primary goal? Am I in it only for monetary gain and no other motive?

      ☐ Or, as a reward? Am I looking for a higher purpose and the money is a reward?

   b) Position

      ☐ As a tool for showing off and self-indulgence? Am I striving for a position to showcase it to the world, proving my importance?

      ☐ Or, as a crown to my achievements and results? Am I striving for a position to showcase my expertise and perseverance in achieving excellence?

   c) Power

      ☐ To rule? Am I striving for power to rule over others? To show my superiority in control of others?

      ☐ Or, to drive positive change? Am I looking for a position of influence and authority to be able to leave a positive mark on the operation and the welfare of employees?

d) Purpose

- ☐ To compensate for my own shortcomings? Am I missing a purpose in life and so compensating?

- ☐ Or, to grow, evolve, and develop? Am I looking for an opportunity to develop myself and the rest of the team?

e) Fulfillment

- ☐ For lack of anything better? This will suffice as this is all I have?

- ☐ Or, confident of my achievements, I feel I have more to achieve, both personally and for the team?

2. What do I strive for?

a) Belonging

- ☐ Due to missing a purpose in life, I want to belong somewhere, anywhere, so this will suffice?

- ☐ Or, due to successful personal development, I feel I have the experience and knowledge to further support the team and company's mission.

b) Respect

- ☐ Based on my personal needs, do I demand and expect respect from everyone?

- ☐ Or, based on experience, I understand that respect is earned and do my best to earn it across the board with my attitude and performance?

c) Results

- ☐ Supporting only my goal? Am I focused only on my results?

- ☐ Or, supporting my goal as it complements the

team's goal? Am I focused on team results complemented by my results?

d) Success

- ☐ My success only? Am I focused on my own glory and not interested in the wider picture?

- ☐ Or, my success within success of a team? Am I focused on achieving success within the team's success?

e) Content

- ☐ With results only? Am I only striving for the final result?

- ☐ Or, with process, results, morale, and preserving integrity? Am I striving for results, driven by the complementing processes, while maintaining my integrity and that of others?

3. How am I getting there?

a) Obey

- ☐ Blindly? Do I question or follow regardless of the consequences to others?

- ☐ Or, do I enforce my considered values and beliefs? Do I analyze the potential consequences and give voice to concerns?

b) Listen

- ☐ Hear, but not listen, and ignore? Do I pretend to listen, but dismiss any input?

- ☐ Or, listen, understand, and incorporate? Do I actively listen to all inputs and decide on the best course of action?

c) Question

- ☐ To demonstrate strength and power? Do I question others to show my importance and authority?

- ☐ Or, to trigger positive change? Do I question others when I see the need and opportunity to elevate everyone's performance and increase productivity supporting my company's mission?

d) Challenge

- ☐ To diminish? Do I challenge people and ideas to diminish others and show superiority?

- ☐ Or to elevate and initiate change for the better? Do I challenge people and ideas to assist in detecting flaws and help in overcoming them?

e) Propose

- ☐ For self-interest? Do I only push myself forward when focusing on my self-interest without regard to others or the company?

- ☐ Or, for a higher purpose? Do I propose changes for everyone's growth and well-being in line with the company's mission?

4. How do I manage people?

a) Instruct

- ☐ Without equipping the team with tools and knowledge? Do I instruct, uninterest in providing the tools and knowledge necessary to achieve the task?

- ☐ Or, offering both tools and knowledge? Do I instruct while making sure all the required tools and knowledge are available, understandable, and acquired?

b) Command

- ☐ Always to stroke my ego? Do I command and show my superiority and power even when not necessary?

- ☐ Or, quietly and when needed due to a specific situation, with vigor tempered with understanding? Do I command in order to achieve positive results in challenging situations? When appropriate, am I not afraid to adopt a strict approach?

c) Direct

- ☐ To serve my goal? Do I issue orders to diminish others when it serves my goal?

- ☐ Or, to achieve the full potential of the team? Am I directing the team to develop and achieve their full potential, both collectively and individually, in a timely manner, while keeping everyone's integrity in mind?

d) Lead

- ☐ Toward the selected goal only? Do I lead only when it serves my chosen, limited goal?

- ☐ Or, always to lead and serve, and bring the best out of the team and all its members?

e) Guide

- ☐ Just in the direction of my success?

- ☐ Or, in the direction of the team and company's success, complemented by my success?

5. How do my colleagues perceive me?

a) Rigid

☐ Due to their misperceptions? Do I see their opinion as a flawed and twisted perception?

☐ Or, due to my flaws? Do I see that perception as an opportunity to self-reflect?

b) Tough

☐ Due to them being weak and needing tough leadership?

☐ Or, due to my strength? Do they perceive me as tough, due to my being stronger in some respects with a tendency to grow, develop, and empower others?

c) Cooperative

☐ Only when achieving my goals? Am I cooperative only when in pursuit of my own goals?

☐ Or, when achieving the team's goal? Am I always cooperative with everyone's best interest in mind?

d) Approachable

☐ When I'm the one in need? Am I approachable when I need a favor back or when hiding an agenda?

☐ Or, always? Am I always approachable and willing to assist and support the common goal?

e) Inspiring

☐ To those who are like-minded and not to the rest of the team?

☐ Or, to everyone? Am I inspiring to all regardless of our differences, as my enthusiasm and approach make them strive for more?

6. How do my subordinates perceive me?

a) Single-minded

- ☐ Suffering a narrow vision due to overload? Am I perceived this way due to my attitude and lack of vision?

- ☐ Or, due to not fulfilling their expectations? Am I perceived this way due to them not getting something from me? Or, perhaps as a quality providing focused leadership?

b) Narrow-minded

- ☐ Due to being overwhelmed by the operation? Am I perceived this way for not being able to accept different points of view and ideas?

- ☐ Or, due to not fulfilling their expectations? Am I perceived this way for not entertaining and supporting their proposed ideas?

c) Fair

- ☐ Because I only support their case when it suits me? Am I only fair to some when doing so supports my self-interest?

- ☐ Or, am I fair across the board, regardless of differences?

d) Enlightening

- ☐ Only to support my own goal? Do I engage in enlightening others only when it is needed to achieve my goal?

- ☐ Or, always, to everyone in my support for the team? Do I encourage everyone in my pursuit of pushing everyone toward success?

e) Visionary

☐ Due to their limitations and lack of vision? Am I perceived this way due to their lack of vision and their limitations?

☐ Or, do I offer real visionary thinking outside of the box? Am I perceived this way because I have fresh ideas and new angles of approach to presented challenges?

7. How do I see myself?

a) ?

b) ?

c) ?

d) ?

e) ?

The purpose!

This questionnaire is not intended to provide a definitive score or right or wrong answers. Its purpose is to encourage you to ask yourself the hard questions and discover your drive, motivation, leadership style, ethical orientation, decision-making approach, and ultimately how you perceive yourself after answering all the questions. It helps you ask the right questions and discover the depths of your inner self.

Take a moment and reflect:

How do you see yourself now?

This is the toughest question, as often we can only see

what we want to see, and it's not necessarily our true self, as it keeps changing and evolving continuously. The perceptions of others will be received in day-to-day interactions or during the performance feedback evaluations.

That is why we need to reflect before, during, and after every action and decision. We want to strive for the optimum at all times. We will have our strengths and weaknesses shaping our leadership style, and working on our strengths without addressing our weaknesses will take us in unwanted directions since we will create narratives to compensate for shortcomings. Such compensation will gradually trim our character and personality and influence our leadership style by changing us as a leader (leader type). We will strive to hide and protect our weaknesses by expressing and exaggerating our strengths, with a profound tendency to perceive potential threats in other people's strengths and, consequently and to the team's detriment, focus on neutralizing them.

This is when we shift from being ourselves to being someone else that we do not necessarily like. It is a true risk, as it slowly creeps in without us even noticing.

So, we need to first identify who we are and then stay true to ourselves, to our purpose and goal. We need to make sure we maintain ourselves and our integrity while performing all duties in our role. We need to stay within our character and belief values and not trade those for peace of mind. If the environment does not support that, perhaps it is time to change the environment. We should protect our integrity and articulate all the challenges we have with any aspect of the operation, management, or company with everyone's best interest in mind. This is the only way to prevent an undesirable culture from infiltrating the company and potentially taking it over. If we realize that our engagement with the company requires bending or completely abandoning our values and beliefs, we need to engage in a deep analysis of the reality and the circumstances in case we succumb to values we cannot respect, and then we must decide on our future employment and engagements within that environment. We always need to change for the better and strive to evolve by accepting all the good influences complementing our values and beliefs, accepting them positively in becoming a better individual, rich in offerings to fellow colleagues and subordinates.

What we should avoid at all costs is losing ourselves and becoming a different person with a character that might potentially not even be accepted by the environment that shaped us. This is our responsibility, and it rests with us not to succumb to (constant) negative influences from multiple directions. We cannot change reality, but we can change how we perceive it and react to it, so we need to make sure we leave our rose-tinted glasses off and see reality as it is to be able to analyze and decide on a well-judged, positive reaction.

APPENDIX 2

Addressing challenges within the team

1. What kind of challenge?

   a) Personal

      ☐ Single employee?

      ☐ Between two employees?

      ☐ Between one or more employees and the majority, or the rest of the team?

   b) Professional

      ☐ Single employee?

      ☐ One segment of the team affected?

      ☐ The whole team affected?

2. How long has the challenge existed?

   a) Existing challenge

      ☐ Existed always, but never addressed?

      ☐ Triggered by previous leadership or a company decision, but never addressed?

   b) Newly presented

      ☐ Just occurred?

      ☐ Just brought to my attention?

3. How does it affect the team?

   a) Cohesion

      ☐ Ruined?

      ☐ Negatively affected?

   b) Performance

      ☐ Affected partially?

      ☐ Negatively affected?

4. Available resources?

   a) Individual

      ☐ Coaching, training, or instruction?

      ☐ Discipline?

   b) Team

      ☐ Meeting?

      ☐ New policy, training, or instruction?

The purpose!

This questionnaire is intended to provide insight into the reasons behind the challenge and help you understand its full complexity, along with the available tools to address it.

2.1 Underperforming employee considerations:

We might have an absolute gem in our hands or just a lost cause. We need to determine the difference and invest time to get the employee to the desired performance level. How easy this might be will depend on everyone involved: the employee, the team, the leader, and the company.

It is important to determine if the underperformance happened before we took over the team or during our leadership. This will give us a clue in which direction to look and which elements to implement.

We need to understand that employees are human beings susceptible to positive and negative influences, with different backgrounds, motivations, and levels of sensibility.

2.1.1 Underperformance continued from the previous leadership:

Obviously, we need to look into the history of performance and actions, if any, taken by the leadership to elevate it. We can approach this with the following steps:

1. **Analyzing an employee's background**

This might seem obvious, or perhaps irrelevant, as the person is employed in a certain role and should perform as expected. We need to understand what previous experiences might have negatively or positively influenced current performance.

This will help us understand the following:

a) Does the employee have advanced skills not being utilized in their current role that might be utilized?

b) Does the employee have previous experiences that could benefit their current position, which might be explored in the spirit of effecting positive change?

c) Does the employee have negative experiences from previous employments preventing them from fully immersing themselves in the role and showcasing their abilities?

This will help us identify potential elements dragging the performance down through the reserved engagement of the employee. If all the answers are negative, then we perhaps do not need to explore further.

Along with their professional background, we should understand their cultural background, which might trigger an underperformance for various reasons. Some examples include working with or under the supervision of individuals belonging to a different religious and cultural group or to the opposite sex. This might sound trivial, but it is a potential friction source, which will not necessarily be voluntarily revealed by the employee due to fear and embarrassment. This is important to understand in any multicultural environment if we are to decide on the right approach to addressing this challenge while embracing all cultural and religious diversity, including opposing views and beliefs.

2. Analyzing an employee's performance review

This is a gold mine, especially when there is a concise process in place that has been adhered to. We will get a lot of information and insight not only on the employee's performance but also on the approach and resolution actions applied by the managers.

This will highlight the following:

a) The employee's performance history with clear indications of fluctuations and areas needing improvement, along with strengths.

b) Was the performance review process adhered to, with all options exhausted in attempts to rectify the performance?

c) If so, which actions were taken to elevate the employee's performance?

d) How did the employee react to the intervention?

e) What was the employee feedback, if captured?

We will determine the history of the underperformance and those behaviors triggering intervention from leadership. This will give us clues into which segments of performance the employee was underperforming and which approaches were taken without the desired results, if any. It then helps us understand if we should focus on a different approach or perhaps on other elements within the performance.

This will also help us identify unsuccessful or even flawed approaches and guide us in a new direction; it might even shed light on a flawed leadership style or a lack of engagement with the challenges in question.

Alternatively, we might discover a flawless five-star employee record that absolutely contradicts reality. This is not unusual as some leaders employ a "participation trophy" approach that rewards anyone who shows up for work with a great performance review in the hope that the actual performance eventually matches it. This then becomes a bit of a challenge, as we need to set the correct standards and expectations. We need to monitor and build a true performance record reflecting accurately the real performance level and providing guidance and feedback in addressing underperformance. Such overoptimistic tactics also reduce a leader's leverage as we do not have a previous history to lean against, so it could well prolong a resolution to the employee's challenges.

3. **Conversation with the employee's colleagues and leaders?**

This is the sensitive part, as we do not ask for opinions, nor should we get them. We are asking for the facts about events, especially from colleagues complaining about the employee. It will give us information regarding the allegations and perceptions of the performance of the employee in question. It is important to maintain the integrity of the process and not succumb to the opinions of other employees and leaders. This process should preferably be integrated with regular conversation and not highlighted as an isolated event to help employees provide honest and uninfluenced testimony. Also, all the information received needs to be taken with a grain of salt and carefully assessed before being taken into consideration. Only facts that can be proven should be considered, with a focus on building our own view of the matter based on the facts received from all available sources. As we have mentioned earlier, there could be tainted opinions from both fellow colleagues and leaders due to cultural differences and unsupportive leadership styles.

4. **Conversation with the employee**

We will conduct this toward the end of the process after getting all the facts together so we can have all questions answered. We need to inform the employee of the nature of the conversation and advise them on their shortcomings while encouraging the employee to express their opinion on the matter, explaining all the circumstances and the chain of events as they recall them. We need to let the employee speak, even if we realize the employee's testimony does not reflect the facts. We need to explain the severity of the employee's actions and advise on the options and tools at our disposal for elevating their performance. We need to advise the employee if the statements do not match facts and allow for explanations. This could lead to a change of testimony or an obdurate sticking with it even when contradicting the facts. It is the employee's right to provide testimony to their best belief, and it needs to be respected; however, we need to make conclusions based on facts.

We need to address all the lessons from the background and performance review evaluation, along with the conversations with the employees and leaders. We then need to express our desire and belief in the employee's ability to deliver an exceptional performance, and, finally, we must offer assistance, tools, and guidance in achieving improvement.

We will obviously focus on the specifics of the underperformance but also highlight the elements that are good, especially those that are elevated, to show our appreciation and respect for a good performance. We are trying to encourage the employee to self-reflect and resolve to produce a better performance with a clear understanding of how to achieve it. We cannot force anyone to change, and, after all, everyone is entitled to live their life as they deem right, including their on-the-job performance. We just need to be clear about company expectations and its readiness to assist in achieving an improvement while respecting everyone's right to refuse help and, consequently, accept the resulting consequences, which must be unequivocally explained.

This needs to be communicated in a clear, direct, and respectful way, establishing a clear understanding of options and consequences.

This approach can lead to one of two outcomes:

1. An identification of hidden and unexplored performance abilities, leading to an elevated performance and employee satisfaction due to respect and understanding of their abilities, by themselves and leaders. Possibly, a newly discovered potential for a different utilization of the employee's abilities and experience.

2. The employee's persistence in underperformance, after exhausting all the opportunities for improvement and intervention from the leadership. This then results in the potential but possibly inevitable separation from the company after continued underperformance and not fulfilling their required tasks at the required level.

Both outcomes are welcome if the process has been exhausted in an attempt to bring the employee's performance to the required level.

Sometimes, we need a push to get us where we need to be, and sometimes, to get away from where we are not supposed to be.

Employees need to understand that they are in charge of their future, and everything depends on their engagement and performance. This is imperative to establish at the beginning, along with set processes and standards of performance evaluation/review and compliance.

We then exhaust the process in an attempt to bring an employee's performance to the desired level and let the employee decide if they are going to honor the contract or not.

And if they do not, then it can go one of two ways:

1. The employee realizes their ability and desire to perform are inadequate to match the required level and they decide to pursue other opportunities.

2. The employee continues to be in denial and accuses everyone else for their shortcomings. There is nothing much we can do at this point, since the person is not responding to all the interventions and refuses to see reality. Whatever we do, the outcome will be the same, so we will need to separate the employee from the company. This will not be taken lightly as

the person is incapable and unwilling to rationalize, perhaps due to personal or professional reasons.

It's as simple as that. We just adhere to the process with the utmost respect for the employee and keep in focus the employee's personal well-being and interests, in line with the company's mission.

2.1.2 Underperformance expressed during our leadership:

This situation presents opportunities to reflect and analyze our leadership style and decisions. We should by now have insight into the background and performance history of all our employees, along with their strengths and weaknesses, which will help us determine directions and considerations when rectifying an undesired performance level by an employee.

We should try to understand the circumstances and get as much feedback from other employees and leaders to gather pertaining facts before speaking with the employee. There could be a situation where there is no additional information we can gather other than the inescapable fact of underperformance. We then need to rely on speaking with the employee to understand the reasons for the lowered performance.

We might determine two main causes for lowered performance in both of the above-mentioned cases:

1. Private
2. Professional

Private: There could be a family situation that dominates the attention and drains the energy of an employee, leaving little or no energy for their job performance. This is something we can have little or no influence on, but we can show respect, understanding, support, and appreciation, which might help the employee gather energy and focus on the things they can control. It then might help the employee with addressing their family affairs, as they will not feel like a failure and will get a boost of enthusiasm from their successful work performance.

Perhaps the employee is dealing with the aftermath of outside elements such as an earthquake or flood, which prevents them from investing the required energy and focusing on the job. We might not be able to solve those challenges, but we might assist in some aspects, such as donations, flexible working hours, or time off work. This will show appreciation and care and will help the employee reorganize and refocus without feeling pressure from both directions.

Professional: This could refer to a missed promotion or a denied request for transfer to another department or position. There might not be much we can assist with, but we can show interest and appreciation while engaging in whatever actions might complement the employee's wishes to help them achieve their ambitions in the future. This will reassure them that the future is bright and the missed opportunity is not going to stop their development and growth.

This could also be due to our leadership style, which triggers a reaction of withdrawal and insecurity in the employee. We need to have honest feedback from the employee and the rest of the team to understand our effect on individual and team performance to help us tailor our approach to get the most out of everyone.

As we mentioned earlier, we can be a source of frustration as we might have deviated from our leadership style without noticing it. So, this presents itself as an opportunity to bring us back on track as well and make the whole team stronger by standing tall, admitting wrong, correcting our approach, and showing appreciation and respect toward all employees. This will empower employees to speak up when needed, which will serve as a self-reflection trigger to address any deviations from our desired leadership style while strengthening the team in their performance and communication and making everyone feel appreciated and respected.

We need to be honest with our employees and direct in delivering good and bad news, but always make an effort to inspire and motivate them to maintain and elevate their performance, even when we cannot influence their desired change within the company.

2.2 Interpersonal challenges and frictions

We will encounter those, perhaps more often than expected. We might have a misunderstanding or perhaps colliding personalities and cultural differences as a trigger. Then again, it could be a rotten apple that is ruining cohesion within the team. We might have one of those individuals who just need drama and conflict.

We need to understand the scale of the event. Is it between two individuals or perhaps a larger section of a team or even the whole team? This sounds easier than it is, especially in a multicultural environment. When we deal with a single culture, it is fairly easy to determine the cultural norm and the spectrum of frictions we might come up against. When we add multiple cultures, it then grows exponentially and makes the combinations of factors almost impossible to apprehend. That is why it is important to understand and put in an effort to get to know all the employees, with their cultural and professional specifics. This is done through conversations, performance feedback, team-building events, recognition, gatherings, and celebrations. It is the relaxed and informal environment that provides us with the best insights into people's true behavior, expectations, and belief systems. They are more relaxed, willing, and open to a conversation revealing cultural and religious specifics and differences. It is also an opportunity to celebrate those differences and point out the common characteristics between cultures.

This should be done to uplift the team's cohesion and strengthen connections between the teammates while accepting and celebrating cultural diversity.

Addressing friction within the team will start with identifying the source and working on rectifying it. We might have two or more colliding views and opinions, in combination with strong personalities not budging. Or perhaps we could have a case of an individual in pursuit of respect. It is important to always approach the situation with an open mind and with the utmost respect for all involved, regardless of how ridiculous the matter might seem. We do not know the true reason until we speak to all involved. Sometimes, it is the fact we got involved that resolves the matter, and no further actions are warranted, and sometimes, we will be counseling several employees to satisfy their need for attention and compassion. Our goal is to build a team, and that is done by showing interest and respect for everyone within the team.

Important aspects to remember:

1. Stay professional

This means you do not get emotionally involved and sucked into the argument. You do not pick sides, and you maintain your integrity. Strengthen your authority by staying professional, maintaining neutrality and keeping everyone involved in line with the company's policies.

2. Maintain focus

You are not the decision maker on the outcome; employees are. They assert discipline when persisting in unprofessional behavior. This is important to remember and to relay to the employees. We do not control this part; they do. Their behavior will get them in trouble, and there will be consequences. Once they realize you are not getting sucked in and becoming part of the argument, but rather you will exercise your authority in line with company standards, policies, and expectations, they will reconsider persisting with their disruption.

You are not their babysitter, nor their parent. They are all adults responsible for their actions. This can be communicated in two ways:

1. Direct and without compassion, which will produce results in most cases, might ruin your rapport with them and cause a rift between you and some employees, especially those who consider themselves to be innocent. So, you should not be stone-cold and uninterested in details but committed only to the resolution.

2. Subtle and involved, which will send the message without affecting your rapport with the team. So, you speak to everyone involved and show interest in their version of events, during which you subtly emphasize everyone's role in the company with the company's expectations with regard to behavior, communication, and respect for others. You draw attention to the operational impact and make them aware of the potential consequences if unacceptable behavior continues. You

empower them to make the right decision while clarifying their understanding of the company's policies, also apprising them of the company's expectations, and providing them a way out by emphasizing a wise approach to ending the friction. This is also a good opportunity to show understanding of their feelings and points of view while emphasizing a focus on their good performance and future achievements.

Sounds elaborate, but the subtle and involved approach is a natural flow and will help you set expectations and put things in perspective without breaking trust and rapport. This approach will allow you to understand what or who is the cause of the friction and help with preventing repetition in the future. It will also set the standard for employee self-coaching, as they understand the outcome will depend on their behavior and participation in the solution rather than the problem.

Is this going to work each time and for everyone? Absolutely not. Some situations will exhaust you and require your full focus and a lot of energy and involvement to come to a reasonable and acceptable resolution. We work with people and they come with a variety of skills, experiences, abilities, and capacity to perceive reality and accept it. This is why it is important to maintain control over yourself and understand your role in the matter while not allowing anyone to control and divert you from it.

A recent meta-analysis of 82 articles, encompassing 104 independent prospective and longitudinal studies with over 30,000 participants (N = 30,314), examined the relationship between destructive leadership and employee outcomes. The study confirmed that destructive leadership negatively impacts employee attitudes and behaviors; surprisingly, it also found that employees' negative behaviors can predict future destructive leadership (Li, Yin, Shi, Damen, & Taris, 2024).[30]

So, yes, you can be a source of frustration and a trigger for negative attitude and behavior in employees, but they can also incite a negative change in your leadership style if you allow yourself to be influenced.

30. Li, P., Yin, K., Shi, J. *et al*. Are Bad Leaders Indeed Bad for Employees? A Meta-Analysis of Longitudinal Studies Between Destructive Leadership and Employee Outcomes. *J Bus Ethics* **191**, 399–413 (2024). https://doi. org/10.1007/s10551-023-05449-2

APPENDIX 3
Performance feedback considerations

3.1 Self Check

3.1.1 Self-check before delivering feedback for poor or below average performance, as part of a disciplinary process:

1. Have I received all the relevant information pertaining to the alleged misconduct, performance or incident?

2. Am I, or have I been, influenced unduly by other employees, colleagues, or upper management opinions?

3. Have I given the employee an opportunity to present their reasoning and circumstances relevant to their performance?

4. Have the explanations received from the employee revealed opportunities for my improvement, or improvement within the company's procedures, policies, and processes?

5. What have I detected as the main reason(s) for the performance?

6. Which mechanisms are at my disposal to address current performance and elevate it in the future?

7. What is the set standard for addressing such a perfor-

mance, and why?

8. Am I making a precedent and why/how?

9. Is my planned action within the company standard and policy?

10. Is my decision going to elevate future performance and help the employee detect and understand opportunities for improvement?

11. Is my decision going to empower the employee to discover strengths and invest in further development, while addressing their weaknesses, in their pursuit of growth, including new opportunities of employment?

3.1.2 Self-check after delivering disciplinary action addressing a poor performance, or feedback on a regular performance:

1. Have I delivered the feedback in such a manner that it empowers the employee to achieve a positive change, avoiding damaging their self-confidence or pushing the employee beyond their limits?

2. Have I captured feedback from the employee and allowed them to express themselves fully and honestly?

3. Have I identified any opportunities for improvement from my side, or pertaining to company policies or procedures?

4. Have I noticed any reason for an increased concern over the employee's well-being?

5. Any signs of distress, or cry for help from the employee?

6. Any sign of changed behavior, especially behavior not

conforming to the employee's norm, indicating a potential shift in the employee's mindset?

We need to understand that it is easy to feel powerful and important when deciding people's futures. We must be cognizant of our tendency to shift toward unwanted behaviors and leadership styles if we are to avoid harming individuals, perhaps even jeopardizing their success in future endeavors.

The tone of feedback and the manner in which we deliver it will have an even greater effect on a person than the actual content of the feedback. This could be either positive or negative, depending on our approach when delivering the feedback. A negative tone could even cause a devastating chain of events and serve as a tipping point, resulting in self-harm or harm to others.

So, we should not refrain from delivering honest feedback with conscientious advice and support, but we need to be mindful of the way we deliver it to minimize negative impacts and potentially catastrophic reactions.

This process could very well be our last opportunity to learn about the circumstances and reasons for the said performance and reveal opportunities for improvement on all sides: the employee, leadership, and the company.

Be a human, not a robot!

3.2 Giving Feedback

3.2.1 Giving positive feedback:

1. Give detailed analysis of all aspects of the performance feedback and explain the set standards.

2. Provide an explanation for each performance section and explain the performance feedback, highlighting where the measurable performance exceeds the expected standard.

3. Emphasize respect and gratitude toward the employee and their performance, emphasizing your clear understanding of the positive impact made on their fellow colleagues and the company.

4. Empower the employee to speak freely regarding any challenges encountered on the road to their excellent performance.

5. Understand the motive and the drive for their excellent performance.

6. Understand the employee's expectations with regards to you and the company.

7. Make sure all questions are answered on both sides, before the feedback session is concluded.

We need to understand the motivation and drive for an outstanding performance and how fragile it might be. What is the risk of it declining in the future, and how can we prevent that from happening and ensure that excellent performance becomes a consistent standard? How can we influence other employees to adopt the preferred performance attitude and standard?

3.2.2 Issuing recognition for an exceptional performance:

1. Emphasize respect and gratitude toward the person and their performance, resulting in a positive impact on their fellow colleagues and our company.

2. Find out from the employee what it is that drives their motivation. Ask whether they see opportunities for improvement with regard to the support available from their fellow colleagues, leadership, and the company.

3. Thank the employee for their exceptional performance, encouraging them to maintain their performance standard.

We need to use this leverage of recognizing when employees deliver results far beyond the average, thereby helping us to imbue this culture for the benefit of all employees across the team.

3.2.3 Giving negative feedback:

1. Give a detailed analysis of all aspects of performance feedback and explain the required standards.

2. Provide explanations for each performance section and explain the delivered performance review with clear and measurable deviations from expected standards.

3. Emphasize respect and gratitude toward the person, but underline a clear understanding of the negative impact on fellow colleagues and the company, emphasizing a belief in their potential capabilities and their ability to improve.

4. Empower the employee to speak up regarding any challenges that negatively affect their performance.

5. Understand the motive and the drive this employee possesses, if any.

6. Understand the expectations held by the employee with regard to you and the company.

7. Provide constructive feedback with clear and measurable expectations, providing access to additional tools to elevate their performance to the required level and within a set time frame.

8. Agree on future performance review periods and expectations to assist in making the set performance level achievable.

9. Make sure all questions are answered on both sides before the feedback session is concluded, establishing a clear understanding by the employee so they may reach out for assistance to achieve their set performance goals.

We need to remember it is our job to exhaust each and every opportunity to improve our employees' performances. We need to treat them with dignity and respect in our pursuit of desirable performances across the board. We need to understand their limitations and organize the opportunities and tools to empower and equip them to succeed before we decide on the final approach and hold them accountable for not achieving the set standard.

3.2.4 Issuing discipline:

1. We need to be convinced that this is the best course of action after exhausting all other possibilities.

2. Give a detailed analysis of all aspects of performance feedback and explain the set standards, along with the different levels of discipline available.

3. Provide explanations for each performance section and the company's disciplinary procedures, and explain the reasons for the disciplinary action, with the employee's clear and measurable performance deviations from the expected standard. Include a documented history of intervention compiled by leadership and colleagues.

4. Emphasize respect and gratitude toward the person, but underline a clear understanding of the negative impact on fellow colleagues and the company, emphasizing a belief in their potential capabilities and their ability to improve.

5. Empower the employee to speak up regarding any challenges that negatively affect their performance

6. Understand the motive and the drive this employee possesses, if any.

7. Understand the expectations of the employee with regard to you and the company.

8. Provide constructive feedback with clear and measurable expectations, providing access to additional tools to rectify the flawed performance and to help elevate performance to the required level within a set time frame.

9. Agree on set periods of performance reviews and the expectations for each to assist in making the set performance level achievable.

10. Make sure all questions are answered on both sides before the feedback session is concluded, establishing a clear understanding by the employee to assist them in reaching out for assistance in achieving their set performance goals.

It is important we handle this particular action in a respectful manner with a clear focus on the well-being of the employee, along with their professional growth and development. We need to understand if the said performance was an isolated deviation from the standard performance and, if so, what the cause was. Was there a history of challenges with the said employee which required deeper analysis and involvement?

The processes highlighted above provide general guidance; obviously, the order of application and the processes themselves, as a whole, should be adapted to fit each specific circumstance if we are to achieve a positive outcome for all.

It is really hard for a leader to have a 100% score of excellent performance reviews or negative performance reviews, as they are managing people across the spectrum of performances influenced by their personal lives, colleagues, leaders, and the company. These fluctuate and shift, so there will be a wide variety of performances throughout the team. Having excellent performances all the time across the board would be highly unusual and a signal that we need to acquire a deeper understanding of the reasons behind it. The same applies to negative performances, as well as an excessive number of disciplinary procedures and separations. These would be indicators of something awry with the leadership approach—too soft or too rigid and authoritarian—and would indicate a need to analyze the reasons.

Also, the company should refrain from creating undue expectations or anxieties around performance feedback, which might prevent leaders from delivering deserved and accurate feedback by adjusting reports to fit company expectations. This could be in both categories, positive and negative. We can come across a company culture where excellent performance ratings are reserved for special circumstances and are issued only rarely. This might make sense from a standard control point of view, but we need to reconsider this approach for two reasons:

1. Leaders might find themselves empowered to rule by fear and focus on bad performances with little or no attention to the mechanism for recognizing and rewarding exceptional performance. Leaders need to be allowed to determine accurate performance levels and should not be restrained from reflecting excellent performances with excellent ratings. This is essential to preserve the integrity and the purpose of the performance delivery process.

2. The employee deserves a performance review that reflects the employee's performance, and they should not be deprived of an accurate picture. This is essential to preserve the employee's motivation and performance level, along with engendering trust in the leadership and the company.

Obviously, we also need to prevent the opposite, where leaders are giving excellent performance ratings to everyone without scrutiny. This is also not good for the reasons below:

1. This would water down the performance delivery process and damage its integrity since there is no incentive to elevate individual performances due to blanket excellent evaluations across the board.

2. It would set an unrealistic expectation in employees, especially amongst those who will become negatively affected when they receive a realistic below-par performance review based on their true performance.

3. It ruins leaders' credibility and lowers personal motivation in employees, who become used to excellent performance reviews regardless of their performance.

4. It paints the wrong picture of individual and team performances, along with the team's readiness to complete its required tasks. This usually comes to light with changes in leadership accompanied by a concomitant implementation of different approaches vis-à-vis performance reviews and their delivery. This can negatively influence the team and cause dissatisfaction, with employees even pushing back against the changes.

We need to find a balance and have the company set the standard for performance reviews and their delivery and hold leaders responsible for the same. We need to refrain from micromanaging this process to prevent potential challenges, as we need to allow leaders the latitude to manage and lead their workforce in line with company standards. If a deviation is noticed, then it needs to be addressed with the responsible leader without compromising the whole process. This can be done through conversation, additional training, or discipline, respectively.

APPENDIX 4
Integration of Artificial Intelligence

W hat is AI? Is it an intelligent entity or written algorithms with instant access to indefinite information provided by humans? Does it learn? Is it capable of making decisions, or is it merely mimicking human logic and reading a cheat sheet made up of a wide variety of information, analyses, decisions, and solutions, constantly being fed and stored in an AI "brain"? Another probably most important question: Is AI considered artificial due to it not being a natural intelligence, and so should it be considered alien, or is it artificial due to not being intelligent at all?

Whatever the answers might be, the fact is it is here to stay, and we should not ignore it. Why? Well, because it will be utilized in every aspect of our lives, and the focus should be on making it complement and advance life rather than helping to destroy it. This might sound like a tinfoil-hat/flat-earth argument influenced by Hollywood movies, but unfortunately, recent history is teaching us differently. We have had opportunities to witness technological advancements utilized for horrific destruction and wars, ranging from black powder to nuclear energy.

So, we need to be realistic and admit that AI does have the potential to be utilized in the most horrific ways, taking us to the point of no return. Whatever we choose to believe, one thing is for sure: it will most definitely influence and change economies by complementing and gradually replacing human beings in a wide variety of jobs and activities.

AI has been born and released "into the wild" by enthusiastic humans, some with personal goals such as financial gain and fame, and some with perhaps "higher" goals aiming at elevating the human race to higher levels of consciousness and speed of information acquisition, processing, and decision-making.

How do we navigate through that?

By way of an example, over the last 100 years, we have seen an increase in the reliability of technology in the aviation industry, where the ratio of technical to human error has changed in favor of technology. So, technology and humans developing it have evolved and advanced to the point of measurable success and reliability, turning those humans that are operating that technology in various segments of the operation into a potential liability. Should we then perhaps remove humans from the equation by having AI operate it too? Absolutely not, although some might desire or even expect it to happen. We are already entering an era of driverless motor vehicles that make decisions in ever-changing environments.

We need to help AI and humans speak the same language and understand one another to be able to complement each other and help minimize errors. AI needs to "understand" the importance of humans and the infinite well of thought, ideas, and solutions hiding in their brains, while humans need to understand the logic and limitations of non-live entities mimicking the human brain without grasping the important aspects of human consciousness, its feelings and souls fueling creativity, continuously guiding them toward extraordinary achievements, including that of AI.

If we fail to do so, we are running the risk of humans becoming a burden to a new society fueled by the expectation of perfection, run by the flawless perception of reality designed by the computer "brain" and uncritically accepted by the cohort of humans in power.

Another challenge is the design of humans with their fragile balance between the urge for constant development and expanding knowledge and the knowledge upkeep. We can see the negative impact on society caused by the development of technology, where previously utilized skills and tools are considered obsolete due to new, more advanced solutions. But the reality is that obsolete skills and tools were the basis for the increasingly advanced skills and tools, and eventually, they become lost for the majority of society, which only relies on and depends on the new. We can see that across industry and in our daily lives with new generations not gaining the skills of the older generations. This gradually turns the majority of society into consumers dependent on technology and designs made by a few rather than maintaining their skills as developers and problem solvers. This has happened throughout history, and now we find ourselves accelerating into the world of AI.

We can approach the above from two different perspectives. One being pro-AI with all the inevitable changes coming as a result of its implementation, its inevitability epitomized perhaps by the argument: should we still be hunting wild animals with primitive tools and living in the caves? We have seen numerous skills and crafts disappear and be replaced by technological advancements that have taken us to where we are today.

Another perspective would be cautious, fearful of the vast potential and the never-before-seen global influence of the new technology on an unimaginable scale if implemented and allowed to develop fully and uncontrollably.

The fear is that AI could reach that level of development and sophistication, pushed by its unfettered enthusiasts, where human employment would become obsolete and AI would "just do its job" as programmed and self-taught automata, the ultimate amoral autodidacts. Then we would find ourselves living in Hollywood movies, the ultimate end-of-day, sci-fi horror where computers apply their final solution to humanity.

Remember: I'll be back!...

Obviously, we have evolved and moved on from primitive society; however, we haven't really addressed the toxic greed polluting all of society. Expecting AI to be immune to such influences is naïve as it is designed by and keeps learning from humans, who have proven throughout history to be flawed and destructive. This is why it is important to set the company's mission, with employees, leadership culture, and all supporting segments of the company, to utilize and exhaust all the positive aspects of technology, including AI, designed to support the growth of the global economy in line with the positive social, cultural, and welfare developments of our society.

Let's make it serve society and not destroy it.

Chapter Checklists

We have discussed various elements of a company, with a primary focus on ethical leadership.

We have established mechanisms for self-check and tools for developing ourselves and others.

We have created a framework that will help us achieve excellence and motivate others to do the same.

Let's use these checklists to assess where we are on this path to excellence and ask ourselves tough questions along the way.

The final and most important question will be:

What can I do differently?

Let's discover that by being rational and honest in answering all these questions.

Chapter 1: Management vs. Leadership

Checklist: Managing Processes or Leading People

- ☐ Is my focus only on processes, or also on employees?

- ☐ Do I see employees only as resources and assets, or as human beings with aspirations, dreams, and dignity?

- ☐ Am I inspiring employees, or just controlling processes?

- ☐ Am I focusing on building new leaders by empowering employees to express themselves and explore their potential?

- ☐ Am I investing time in understanding employees and exploring their unique skills?

Chapter 2: Mission & Vision

Checklist: Mission & Vision Alignment Questions

- ☐ Are our Mission & Vision achievable and realistic?
- ☐ Do they explain why we exist as a company?
- ☐ Do they explain where we're going as a company?
- ☐ Do they align with and support ethics and societal benefit?
- ☐ Can every employee understand and align with them?
- ☐ Have they been safeguarded against flawed systems and decision-making?
- ☐ Have they been assessed against realistic influences?
- ☐ Are they safeguarded against future misalignment with social and ethical norms?

Chapter 3: Business Legal Framework

Checklist: Business Guardrail

- ☐ Have we identified all relevant laws and regulations?
- ☐ Do we have systems in place to monitor changes in laws and regulations?
- ☐ Are we maintaining direction that supports the company's Mission & Vision?
- ☐ Are we allowing for incubation of new ideas in line with the company's Mission & Vision?
- ☐ Have we established transparent two-way communication with both employees and the public?
- ☐ Does the company's public image reflect our Mission & Vision?
- ☐ Are marketing efforts aligned with the company's Mission & Vision and protected from external influences such as lobbyists, political pressure, or temporary shifts in social consensus?

Chapter 4: Standard

Checklist: Operational Standard

☐ Is the company's standard aligned with its Mission & Vision?

☐ Is the company's standard based on competence and true operational needs and not box-ticking?

☐ Is it assessed and updated accordingly when laws, regulations, tools, or technology and market supply/demand change?

☐ Are new training and certification requirements essential?

☐ Are new equipment, protocols, and procedures essential?

☐ Was the standard created from the bottom up with a clear understanding of specific requirements for each position and process?

☐ Did employees contribute to shaping the standard?

☐ Is the standard regularly reassessed with up-to-date input from the employees?

Chapter 5: Compliance Process

Checklist: Trust-Based Compliance Model

- ☐ Is the compliance process transparent?
- ☐ Is documentation clear and easily accessible?
- ☐ Do audits focus on discovering opportunities for improvement rather than assigning blame?
- ☐ Are communication and trust maintained between employees and the compliance team?
- ☐ Is record keeping established, monitored, and protected from tampering and abuse?
- ☐ Is the compliance team competent, motivated, and qualified to deliver audits aimed at discovering opportunities for improvement?
- ☐ Is the compliance process safeguarded against distortion, self-promotion, or abuse of power?

Chapter 6: Hiring

Checklist: Hiring Process

- ☐ Have we defined the hiring process?
- ☐ Does it support our company's Mission & Vision?
- ☐ Have we identified the skills needed for each role?
- ☐ Have we established job descriptions and standards required to maintain excellence?
- ☐ Are compliance and legal requirements included in the process?
- ☐ Have we identified the hiring agent skill set required to execute the hiring process in line with our company's Mission & Vision?
- ☐ Have we decided whether to use an in-house hiring team or outsource?
- ☐ If outsourced, have we communicated expectations and standards aligned with our company's Mission & Vision?
- ☐ Have we established a feedback process to capture signals for change regarding each segment of the hiring process?
- ☐ Have we established a succession planning process and ensured it is safeguarded from misuse and distortion?

Chapter 7: Feedback

Checklist: Performance Feedback Process

- ☐ Have we defined the performance feedback framework?
- ☐ Did it capture crucial individual or group tasks?
- ☐ Have we established a performance feedback form and process?
- ☐ Is it clear, unambiguous, and accessible by both the leaders and the employees?
- ☐ Does it serve as a record keeper and is it protected from tampering, abuse, and manipulation?
- ☐ Have we established performance feedback delivery and expectations?
- ☐ Have we established regular feedback intervals?
- ☐ Have I prepared feedback using facts rather than emotions?
- ☐ Have I delivered feedback privately and respectfully?
- ☐ Have I included recognition and not just critique?
- ☐ Have I checked for understanding and defined next steps?
- ☐ Have I received employee feedback, including the appeal?

Chapter 8: Leadership Styles

Checklist: Red Flag Awareness Guide

- ☐ Do I have the required skills for the position?
- ☐ Am I enthusiastic and passionate in my role?
- ☐ Are there any opportunities for my improvement?
- ☐ Am I compensating for gaps in knowledge or skill?
- ☐ Am I hiding behind the position of authority?
- ☐ Do I motivate and encourage employees to advance their performance?
- ☐ Do I withhold information as a form of dominance?
- ☐ Do I use authority to serve or to dominate?
- ☐ Do I divide and rule?
- ☐ Do I encourage open dialogue?
- ☐ Do I support toxic culture through favoritism?
- ☐ Are my decisions transparent?
- ☐ Do I acknowledge and reward excellence?
- ☐ Do I support employee development and growth?
- ☐ Do I recognize potential in employees and support further advancement and development?
- ☐ Do I foster open, two-way communication?

Chapter 9: Leader Types

Checklist: Self-Diagnostic: Which Leader Am I?

- [ ] **Do I say, "Follow me"?**
- [ ] Do I lead by example?
- [ ] Do I serve my team?
- [ ] Do I strengthen my team?
- [ ] Do I understand the strengths and weaknesses of my team members?
- [ ] Do I protect my team?
- [ ] Do I admit when I am wrong and rectify it?
- [ ] **Do I say, "Wasn't me"?**
- [ ] Do I avoid certain responsibilities?
- [ ] Do I aim to just get by rather than excel in my role?
- [ ] Do I avoid raising flags due to self-preservation?
- [ ] **Do I act like, "I'm not here"?**
- [ ] Do I avoid all responsibility?
- [ ] Do I focus on self-promotion regardless of others?
- [ ] Do I divide a team and exploit individuals for personal promotion?
- [ ] Do I fail to recognize good performance but issue harsh discipline for underperformance?

Chapter 10: Attitudes

Checklist: Personal Attitude Lens

- ☐ **Do I strive for excellence?**
- ☐ Am I focused and quick in problem resolution?
- ☐ Do I sometimes fail to recognize when to quit?
- ☐ Am I difficult to follow in my pursuit of excellence?
- ☐ **Do I seek purpose?**
- ☐ Do I prioritize belonging over performance?
- ☐ Do I abandon my beliefs to fit into the company culture?
- ☐ Is my need to belong greater than my urge to address concerns with the company?
- ☐ **Do I just ride along?**
- ☐ Do I consider myself overqualified and underchallenged in this position?
- ☐ Do I consider myself underqualified and overwhelmed in this position?
- ☐ Which attitude currently dominates within my team?
- ☐ How do I shift from a "Just in it for a ride" attitude to a "Looking for purpose" or "Striving for excellence" attitude?

Chapter 11: Combinations

Checklist: Leader Type with a Personal Attitude

- [ ] **Am I a "Follow me" leader with a "Striving for excellence" attitude?**
- [ ] Am I shooting for the stars?
- [ ] Am I leading my team and my company in a direction of success?
- [ ] Am I taking ownership of the situation and bringing others along?
- [ ] Is the well-being of my entire team a priority to me?
- [ ] **Am I a "Wasn't me" leader with a "Looking for purpose" attitude?**
- [ ] Am I dependent on the leading forces?
- [ ] Am I under the umbrella of my leader?
- [ ] Am I always waiting for approval to act?
- [ ] **Am I an "I'm not here" leader with a "Just in it for a ride" attitude?**
- [ ] Am I offering a problem for every solution, while holding back my team's performance?
- [ ] Am I allowing my personal life to negatively influence my professional performance?
- [ ] How do I shift toward a "Follow me" leader with a "Striving for excellence" attitude?

Chapter 12: Company Culture

Checklist: Culture Health Questions

- ☐ Do we reward integrity over shortcuts?
- ☐ Do we cherish diversity in values and beliefs?
- ☐ Do we empower everyone to achieve their full potential?
- ☐ Is our company culture built on mutual respect, not fear?
- ☐ Are promotions linked to competence rather than politics?
- ☐ Does our prevailing leadership style model the company culture we want?
- ☐ **Is our culture a "Leader cult" culture?**
- ☐ Do we promote unquestioned authority?
- ☐ Are we preventing employees from speaking up due to fear of repercussions?
- ☐ **Is our culture a "The end justifies the means culture"?**
- ☐ Do we prioritize results over integrity and the well-being of employees?
- ☐ Is the bottom line our only motivation?
- ☐ Does our goal justify any means to achieve it?
- ☐ **Is our culture a "Quid pro quo culture"?**
- ☐ Do we support favoritism?
- ☐ Do we tolerate harassment or bullying within our teams?

Chapter 13: Conclusion

Checklist: Shared Responsibility Compass

- ☐ **Has our company** created a culture that cherishes creativity, ingenuity, excellence, perseverance, and dedication while celebrating differences and personal dignity?

- ☐ Has it established standards, trainings, processes, systems, and resources?

- ☐ Is it serving the greater good of society while preserving the environment?

- ☐ **Have our leaders** developed teams and future leaders by inspiring and supporting growth while preserving dignity and integrity?

- ☐ Have we established clear and undistorted communication with the team?

- ☐ Have we communicated all deficiencies and suggestions for improvement promptly?

- ☐ **Have our employees** upheld standards and contributed to culture?

- ☐ Have they delivered their best performance and suggested improvements?

- ☐ **Have we, together,** built a sustainable and resilient organization that serves society and protects human dignity?

References

References & Further Reading

1. https://www.marineinsight.com/marine-safety/the-relation-between-human-error-and-marine-industry/#:~:text=These%20studies%20were%20aimed%20at%20finding%20out%20root,the%20reason%20for%20maritime%20accidents%20was%20human%20error

2. https://www.faasafety.gov/files/gslac/courses/content/258/1097/AMT_Handbook_Addendum_Human_Factors.pdf

3. https://www.justice.gov/opa/pr/justice-department-announces-largest-health-care-fraud-settlement-its-history

4. https://www.justice.gov/opa/pr/johnson-johnson-pay-more-22-billion-resolve-criminal-and-civil-investigations

5. https://www.merriam-webster.com/dictionary/kickback

6. https://www.justice.gov/opa/pr/pharmaceutical-giant-astrazeneca-pay-520-million-label-drug-marketing

7. https://www.investopedia.com/articles/economics/08/government-financial-bailout.asp

8. https://en.wikipedia.org/wiki/List_of_oil_spills

9. https://en.wikipedia.org/wiki/List_of_largest_pharmaceutical_settlements

10. https://www.epa.gov/pfas/pfas-explained

11. https://www.theguardian.com/environment/2023/aug/03/chemical-companies-pfas-payouts-forever-chemicals

12. https://www.nytimes.com/2016/04/23/business/international/volkswagen-loss-emissions-scandal.html

13. https://en.wikipedia.org/wiki/Subprime_mortgage_crisis

14. https://www.justice.gov/opa/pr/volkswagen-engineer-sentenced-his-role-conspiracy-cheat-us-emissions-tests

15. https://www.consumerreports.org/cars/car-reliability-owner-satisfaction/electric-vehicles-are-less-reliable-than-conventional-cars-a1047214174/

16. https://www.reuters.com/business/autos-transportation/carmakers-adjust-electrification-plans-ev-demand-slows-2024-09-06/

17. https://www.businessinsider.com/automakers-rolling-back-electric-car-plans-porsche-honda-jeep-ford-2025-9#ford-6

18. https://www.reuters.com/business/autos-transportation/stellantis-toyota-ford-mazda-subaru-plan-pool-co2-emissions-with-tesla-2025-01-07/

19. https://www.nytimes.com/2024/01/17/business/tesla-charging-chicago-cold-weather.html

20. https://www.usatoday.com/story/money/2025/08/27/cracker-barrel-logo-change-timeline/85845032007/

21. https://www.nytimes.com/2022/09/08/us/oberlin-bakery-lawsuit.html

22. https://about.fb.com/news/2025/01/meta-more-speech-fewer-mistakes/

23. https://www.cbsnews.com/news/meta-dei-programs-mcdonalds-walmart-ford-diversity/

24. https://www.foxbusiness.com/politics/meta-policy-chief-says-decision-end-dei-ensures-company-hires-the-most-talented-people

25. https://www.congress.gov/bill/118th-congress/senate-bill/4516/text

26. https://www.mitma.gob.es/recursos_mfom/2012costaconcordia.pdf

27. https://www.investopedia.com/terms/e/enron.asp

28. https://en.wikipedia.org/wiki/Sexual_harassment_in_the_workplace_in_the_United_States

29. https://www.eeoc.gov/data/sexual-harassment-our-nations-workplaces

30. https://rdcu.be/eQoom
    Li, P., Yin, K., Shi, J. *et al.* Are Bad Leaders Indeed Bad for Employees? A Meta-Analysis of Longitudinal Studies Between Destructive Leadership and Employee Outcomes. *J Bus Ethics* **191**, 399–413 (2024).https://doi.org/10.1007/s10551-023-05449-2

Further Reading Recommendations

Book mentioned for context or reference:

Grebenar, Vladimir – *Isus Lider*

Afterword

L eadership is a lifelong journey and an exciting one with lots of ups and downs, but ultimately rewarding in ways that are hard to achieve by any other means. It is a privileged position of influence and, one could say, power that allows you to make positive changes not only in your professional journey but also in your private life, along with the professional and private lives of your colleagues and subordinates.

We have scratched the surface of leadership in this book, as a book embracing the whole concept would be indefinite.

I hope you have learned something new and received new angles on the matter, with perhaps even an unorthodox approach to understanding challenges that come with leadership along with a variety of tools for tackling them.

One thing you need to take away from this experience is the importance of You. You are going to make it or break it. You are going to change the world, but only by changing yourself.

So, let me thank you for your patience and dedication in finishing this book and invite you to further development in support of your positive change and growth by joining our leadership community at www.icsoultuons.blog, with additional development resources at your disposal.

About the author

Zoran Vidovic has an interesting career path spanning from the hospitality industry to the military and marine sector, where he held leadership positions and made a positive influence with measurable results, followed by entrepreneurship in hospitality real estate.

His military career is a testimony of resilience and dedication, which was rewarded with officer rank and commendation from the commander of the Croatian Army for delivering exceptional services as a reconnaissance platoon commander.

Zoran further developed his skills in close protection and enrolled in the marine security sector, serving as chief security officer on Disney Cruise Linc vessels. His expertise was utilized during new builds and dry docks, where he was entrusted with critical security activities and development, including the design and installation of vessel locking plans, ship security plans, and assessments, along with other highly sensitive procedures and processes.

With a diploma in economics, the author turned vision and leadership into a real estate success story. Zoran enrolled in hospitality real estate development, designing and building successful real estate, turning personal investment into a hospitality asset with a 1,060% ROI.

His passion for teaching and developing leaders has led him to found the I.C.Solutions.blog, where he addresses leadership challenges in his blog posts and offers leadership coaching and consulting with practical advice and thought leadership on topics such as:

- Effective leadership styles
- Navigating workplace conflict
- Building team trust and cohesion
- Crisis and risk management
- Personal development for leaders

He is passionate about helping existing and new leaders and entrepreneurs with leadership challenges with the intention of empowering leaders to become the best versions of themselves in an effort to serve society.

Your time invested in this book is sincerely appreciated. I hope it has inspired reflection and supported your journey of personal development.

If you'd like to share your thoughts, please leave a review by scanning the QR code below.

Your feedback helps others discover the book and contributes to the broader conversation on responsible leadership.

With appreciation,

Zoran Vidović

www.ingramcontent.com/pod-product-compliance
Lightning Source LLC
LaVergne TN
LVHW052024080426
835513LV00018B/2146